DOMINO

A PLAY

By
ROBERT LITZ

SAMUEL FRENCH, INC.
45 WEST 25TH STREET NEW YORK 10010
7623 SUNSET BOULEVARD HOLLYWOOD 90046
LONDON TORONTO

ISBN 0 573 69089 8 Printed in U.S.A.

IMPORTANT BILLING AND CREDIT REQUIREMENTS

All producers of DOMINO *must* give credit to the Author of the Play in all programs distributed in connection with performances of the Play and in all instances in which the title of the Play appears for purposes of advertising, publicizing or otherwise exploiting the Play and/or a production. The name of the Author *must* also appear on a separate line, in which no other name appears, immediately following the title, and *must* appear in size of type not less than fifty percent the size of the title type.

Cover Artwork by Marty Luko.

"DOMINO" was first presented in New York as a reading by Primary Stages on December 10, 1987. Directed by Fritz Ertl with:

Eddie Jones .... ROGERS
Larry Pine .... LANGLEY
Ernesto Gonzalez .... NUEVA
Mark Diekmann .... MAHAN
Michael Morin .... CADRE
Dennis Fox .... MAN
Christine Mauricio .... WOMAN

"DOMINO" was presented as part of the PlayLab series of Arena Stage in Washington, D.C., on March 6, 1988. Dramaturg, Lloyd Rose. Directed by James C. Nicola with:

Jerry Whiddon .... ROGERS
Terrence Currier .... LANGLEY
Carlos Gonzalez .... NUEVA
Henry Strozier .... MAHAN
Jorge Abreu .... CADRE
Raoul N. Rizik .... MAN
Desiree Marie .... WOMAN
Sarah Marshall .... (directions)

"DOMINO" opened Off Broadway at the Perry Street Theatre, in New York, produced by New York Theatre Workshop. on April 20, 1988. James Nicola, Artistic Director. Directed by David Esbjornson, with:

Jay Patterson .... ROGERS
Dan Butler.............................. LANGLEY
Jaime Sanchez.............................. NUEVA
Christopher McHale...................... MAHAN
Socorro Santiago.......................... WOMAN
Raoul Rizik .... MAN
Carlos Cestero............................ CADRE

Sets, Elizabeth Doyle; Costumes, Marianne Powell-Parker; Lights, Greg MacPherson; Sound, Lia Vollack; Production Stage Manager, Dan M. Weir; Production Manager, Darrien Lee Cole; Managing Director NYTW, Nancy Kassak Diekmann.

CHARACTERS

ROGERS, (the Banker) loan officer for a major International Bank.

LANGLEY, (Station Chief) of an unnamed American agency.

NUEVA, (the General) top military man of an unnamed Central American "republic."

MAHAN, (the Advisor) an American military/intelligence "advisor" to the oft-mentioned unnamed "republic."

WOMAN, a Central American woman of mixed breeding who plays a variety of roles and who dies once.

MAN, a Central American man, also of mixed blood playing many roles, who dies three times.

CADRE, (the Revolutionary) a young revolutionary leader who refuses to recognize the legitimacy of any Central American "republic" or its officials. Nonetheless, a true pragmatist.

TIME

The present.

PLACE

An unnamed country in Central America.

SCENE BREAKDOWN

1. *Southern Exposures*
   Rogers; Langley; Mahan

2. *Putting Around*
   Rogers; Langley; Nueva

3. *Due Diligence*
   Woman; Rogers; Nueva; Mahan

4. *The Other Economy*
   Langley; Mahan

5. *Rancho del Banco*
   Man; Woman; Cadre; Rogers; Langley; Nueva

6. *Yes, We Have Bananas*
   Man; Woman; Cadre; Rogers; Langley; Nueva

7. *Name, Rank, and American Express Number*
   Rogers; Cadre; Man; Woman

8. *Double Espresso*
   Langley; Nueva; Mahan; Cadre

9. *Behind the "Veil"*
   Rogers; Nueva; Mahan; Man

10. *Drinks on the House*
    Rogers; Woman; Man

11. *Spoils of War*
    Cadre; Man; Woman

12. *Southern Air Transport*
Rogers; Man; Woman; Cadre; Langley

13. *After the Ball*
Langley; Nueva

*If an intermission is felt to be necessary, it should occur between scenes 13 and 14.

14. *P.S., Send Fresh Underwear*
Man; Rogers; Cadre

15. *Marionettes*
Langley; Rogers; Cadre

16. *Nocturnal Visitors*
Cadre; Man; Woman; Langley; Mahan

17. *Confiteor Omne Peccata Mea*
Nueva; Man; Woman

18. *The Big Picture*
Mahan; Cadre

19. *Let's Make a Deal*
Langley; Cadre; Rogers

20. *Photo Opportunity*
Nueva; Woman; Langley

21. *Big Fish, Little Fish,* or "My Dinner with Cadre"
Rogers; Cadre; Langley; Man

22. *Pulling Strings*
Mahan; Nueva

23. *Dominos*

Nueva; Mahan; Langley; Cadre; Man; Woman

PRODUCTION NOTE

Scene "titles" should be used. One possibility is to display these titles on a moving electronic ticker which quotes stock prices on the world's markets at different times during the play, in preset, and between scenes. "The End" could therefore be indicated by "Market Closed."

Scene 1
Southern Exposures

ROGERS scans a financial prospectus. MAHAN stands guard at door. He remains a silent, unblinking presence, more than less ignored by ROGERS and LANGLEY in briefing room.

ROGERS. FUCK 'EM! *(long pause)*

LANGLEY. Nevertheless ... with the coca crop down sixty-five, cocoa down twenty, and coffee—

ROGERS. I said fuck 'em!!!

LANGLEY. Right. *(pause)*

ROGERS. Cocoa's down sixty-five?

LANGLEY. Co*ca*.

ROGERS. Coca's not even listed.

LANGLEY. Depends whose list you're checking.

ROGERS. And our list says sixty-five.

LANGLEY. Yes. *(pause)*

ROGERS. And cocoa's down twenty.

LANGLEY. Right. *(slight pause)*

ROGERS. What's coffee?

LANGLEY. Ten.

ROGERS. Up or down?

LANGLEY. Down.

ROGERS. Then they're fucked anyway.

LANGLEY. Not quite.

ROGERS. They're fucked in coffee, coca, and cocoa. They don't HAVE anything else.

LANGLEY. Yes they do.

ROGERS. What? Tourism? Gimme a break. They got — what? — ten hotels, one casino, a couple pools, ten dollar buck-a-disease whores, and one golf course. You ever play it?

LANGLEY. I don't play. Golf.

ROGERS. I've seen better bean fields!

LANGLEY. It was.

ROGERS. What was what?

LANGLEY. The golf course. A beanfield. They threw the peasants out and put in a clubhouse and an eighteen-hole course.

ROGERS. Clubhouse. Yeah, right. Locker room with attached garage.

LANGLEY. It's not tourism.

ROGERS. You can bet your sweet ass it ain't. Tourism there's a joke. You can't even trade their fuckin' money. It's not good anywhere. Half the time it's not even good there!

LANGLEY. Exactly.

ROGERS. Okay, so what is it? And don't tell me "oil."

LANGLEY. Debt.

ROGERS. Debt?

LANGLEY. Debt. Three point six billion's worth. And that's just to us. The Europeans—

ROGERS. Are fucked.

LANGLEY. Precisely. *(pause)*

ROGERS. So if the Europeans are fucked — and believe

me, they are fucked — what about us?

LANGLEY. You want this in terms you can understand?

ROGERS. Yes, I want it in terms I can understand.

LANGLEY. You're fucked. *(After a beat, ROGERS Exits. When LANGLEY turns to MAHAN, he finds MAHAN trying to place his face.)*

MAHAN. Angola, right? *(then off LANGLEY'S look)* Grenada. *(LANGLEY just smiles.)* Wait a minute. Wait ... a ... minute. I got it. Phnom Penh, '73.

LANGLEY. We weren't *in* Cambodia.

MAHAN. Right.

LANGLEY. Your pal, the bird colonel with the bad ear and the tattoo of Siva on his left pec sends his best.

MAHAN. Bei—rut! Hot damn!

LANGLEY. Tire smoke, tear gas, and a buncha hot-wired ragheads tossing frags — nice change of pace. You woulda loved it. Been South?

MAHAN. Some. But it ain't nothin' like the "rute."

LANGLEY. Getting hot down there?

MAHAN. Must be if they're sending you back in. *(LANGLEY smiles. Pause.)*

LANGLEY. You don't know a goddam thing about me.

MAHAN. Well ... I just assumed—

LANGLEY. Not a good idea, friend. *(slight pause)* Lots of curious congressional eyes'll be looking our way. This ain't Laos. No "recreational" kills. C'mon. I'll brief you over a couple or six brewskies. San Miguel's your pleasure, ain't it?

MAHAN. That's in my file, too?

LANGLEY. I like details.

MAHAN. So let's do it.

LANGLEY. One thing.

MAHAN. Yeah?

LANGLEY. *(suddenly very military)* I say jump, you don't even ask how high, you just do it.

MAHAN. *(saluting)* Sir. Yes, sir.

LANGLEY. I think you're gonna work out just fine. Here. Have a few. *(LANGLEY hands him a plane ticket and cash in an envelope then starts to Exit. He stops at the door.)* See you Tuesday in Tegoose.

End of Scene 1

Scene 2
Putting Around

LANGLEY "tests" ROGERS' putter. They are in ROGERS' office.

LANGLEY. Never quite developed a taste for the game.

ROGERS. Look, our exposure's already so deep we can't afford to reschedule the loans without some guarantees.

LANGLEY. Such as?

ROGERS. "Underwriting."

LANGLEY. When they *(NUEVA)* borrow a little, it's their problem. When they borrow a lot, it's *your (ROGER'S, the banks)* problem ... You lent too much, too fast. You were dumb. Now you want us to bail you out?

ROGERS. We're not talking Chrysler here, Amigo. When they borrow a lot, it's our problem. When they borrow too much, it becomes *your* problem.

LANGLEY. Maybe.

ROGERS. Bullshit maybe. If the house collapses, the rubble's on your lot.

LANGLEY. But when this financial market collapses there will still be governments. But banks? Your bank? Probably not.

(NUEVA Enters.)

LANGLEY. Ah, General. Welcome to New York.

ROGERS. He's late.

LANGLEY. The General is a very busy man.

ROGERS. I'm not?

NUEVA. Everything settled?

LANGLEY. Just a few minor details.

ROGERS. If they want our money, he'll be ... nice. *(LANGLEY hands NUEVA the putter. ROGERS starts to object, LANGLEY cautions him. Throughout the rest of the scene, NUEVA continues to putt a golf ball on the "carpet" of the office.)*

NUEVA. You'll give it regardless.

ROGERS. We'll see about that. *(ROGERS starts to leave.)*

LANGLEY. Oh sit down.

ROGERS. I don't have to take this.

NUEVA. No?

ROGERS. No. *(Exits.)*

NUEVA. He'll be back.

LANGLEY. Eventually. *(Pause. NUEVA twirls and holds the putter as though it were either a walking stick or commander's baton.)*

NUEVA. We've talked to our friends.

LANGLEY. In a sinking boat, my friend, nobody is a friend.

NUEVA. If we all pull together — pooling our indebtedness ... What is good for all is good for each.

LANGLEY. Solidarity.

NUEVA. Yes.

LANGLEY. Unity.

NUEVA. Forever!

LANGLEY. But whoever breaks from the group first gets the best deal. *(slight pause)* And here you are. Alone.

NUEVA. *(faint smile)* Of course.

(ROGERS Re-enters. NUEVA resumes putting.)

ROGERS. Let's deal.

NUEVA. *(without looking up)* For whom do you speak?

ROGERS. Myself.

NUEVA. And the other banks?

ROGERS. I'm here, they're not. *(pause)* Rescheduling is ... a possibility. *(slight pause)* A *genuine* possibility. *(NUEVA continues putting.)* I could just say "no" just like everybody else.

NUEVA. You won't.

ROGERS. Don't be so sure.

NUEVA. In prison-poker, the weak always blink. You'll blink. And like it.

ROGERS. Like hell I will. *(NUEVA looks up from the putt and engages in a stare-down with ROGERS. ROGERS blinks, naturally. NUEVA "calls" him on it.)* I didn't blink. I did not blink! These people have no discipline! They're sloppy! Lazy! Greedy! *(ROGERS fumes. NUEVA checks the "lay" with his putter, holding it as a plumb then going down to knees.)* What's he looking for? "Subversives?"

NUEVA. For a level spot ... suitable for landing military aircraft. *(slight pause)* We are a poor country. Our major industry is harboring subversives and illiterate caddies.

ROGERS. We've already given you four billion.

NUEVA. And we have paid you back three billion two hundred million.

ROGERS. Interest, mostly.

NUEVA. Three point two billion. Dollars! You lend us money to pay the interest. You show profits, we get deeper into debt. We know what your stockholders think about your bad loans. But what will they say if we were unable to continue to borrow in order to pay? What will they say if we are *unwilling* to pay?

ROGERS. Countries don't go bankrupt.

NUEVA. They nationalize.

ROGERS. Do that and you'll never see another dollar, mark, franc, pound or yen.

NUEVA. There are always rubles. *(to LANGLEY:)* Yes?

LANGLEY. "They" won't be so ... understanding.

NUEVA. Is he *(ROGERS)*? *(NUEVA throws the putter at*

ROGER'S ankles. ROGERS leaps away.)

ROGERS. You dirty little...

NUEVA. One hundred from you *(LANGLEY)*. Two hundred from you *(ROGERS)*. For now. Good faith.

ROGERS. *(muttered)* Fat chance.

LANGLEY. And the object of these funds?

NUEVA. *(picking up the golfball)* Infrastructure.

ROGERS. Such as?

NUEVA. Ball washers. *(NUEVA tosses the ball to ROGERS then Exits laughing. Slight pause.)*

ROGERS. Why throw good money after bad?

LANGLEY. Because, if you don't, your money won't be good anywhere. Not ever here. *(LANGLEY hands ROGERS an envelope with plane tickets.)* Pan Am. Flight 117. Clipper Class okay?

ROGERS. Terrific. He flies First Class and I get—

LANGLEY. First Class. On the way back. By the way...

ROGERS. What?

LANGLEY. I've got a little cash I'd like you to move down to your branch. Nothing major. A couple mil. Petty cash, really. For expenses. Park it in the Caymans overnight, okay?

ROGERS. Why should I?

LANGLEY. Because we're all in this together, right? I mean, hey, we both gotta play the cards we draw. I don't like this guy any more than you do. But he's the only game in town. For now. I gotta tell you, I feel damn lucky — pretty goddam lucky — I've got you in my corner. I like your style. It's ... "ballsy." Tell you what — fuck it — First Class, all the way. Nothing but the best.

ROGERS. The Hilton?

LANGLEY. I prefer the International, but if the Hilton's what you want...

ROGERS. Make it a suite. ... At the International.

End of Scene 2

Scene 3
Due Diligence

A peasant WOMAN in ragged clothes and straw hat Enters, toting an enormous golf bag. She slowly crosses under its grave burden, Exiting opposite. Pause. ROGERS Enters in his la turista outfit, jauntily swinging his driver. Accompanying him, dressed in a crisp military uniform, sporting mirror shades and a chromed sidearm is NUEVA. ROGERS is in great good humor.

ROGERS. I remember back in — Christ, it must've been '73 — the boss sent me and a whole gaggle of kids right out of the B-School globe-trotting to every two-bit, mule 'n a half country south of Houston. Anastasio and me, and I think it was his brother or cousin-in-law or something, and this little prick from Chase got in a round down in San Jose. You ever get down there? Helluva layout...

(They Exit. Pause. The WOMAN/CADDY Re-enters and begins a

slow cross. Just before she is about to Exit, ROGERS and NUEVA Re-enter. ROGERS now has his five iron out, twirling it with casual ease. By the middle of ROGERS' following speech, the WOMAN has Exited.)

ROGERS. So for three friggin' hours the little prick from Chase will talk nothing but GNP this, GDP that, leading indicators, amortized assets, floating rates, Eurodollars, Petrodollars ya-di-ya-di-ya til Stazi — that's what I called him, Stazi — was ready to tell his bodyguard to garrot the son of a bitch. And all the while the little prick is trying to hustle off a loan to the Generalissimo, all the "Big G" wants to know is real estate prices in Miami and which Zurich banker he should see. Did some good business that day. Shot a seventy-nine, with a double-bogey on the back. *(Almost steps on his ball.)* Where in the hell is she going?!! Hey! YO! Senorita!!! What the hell's her name again?

NUEVA. Juan.

ROGERS. Can't be. She's a she.

NUEVA. Everybody's name is "Juan."

ROGERS. C'mon.

NUEVA. Try it.

ROGERS. *(after a pause)* Yo! Juan!!!

(The WOMAN Enters.)

ROGERS. You walked right past my ball! Ball! What the hell's the word for "ball"?

NUEVA. "Bola."

ROGERS. I thought that meant "revolution." *(NUEVA shrugs. ROGERS eyes him suspiciously. ROGERS points to the golf ball on the ground.)* This is my BOLA! *(The WOMAN suddenly looks very worried, searching on all sides.)* It's right here, dummy!!! *(ROGERS points to the ball summoning the peasant woman.)* Jeez. Give me my ... nine iron. NINE IRON. NUEVE! *(The WOMAN hands ROGERS a six iron.)* That's a six. SIX! *(Infuriated, he grabs the club out of the bag himself. NUEVA studies the surrounding area and quietly unholsters his handgun. ROGERS addresses his ball, waggling for a long time to get back his concentration. Just as he starts into his downswing, NUEVA fires off a round upstage. ROGERS cracks; his grip loose, the swung club goes flying off stage left. The peasant WOMAN dives for cover behind the golfbag at the sound of the GUNFIRE erupting in the distance. ROGERS, frightened:)* What? What was that? *(NUEVA Exits. The WOMAN starts to crawl away, then flees at the "war cry" of a man charging onto the stage. ROGERS howls, trying to hide behind the golfbag.)*

(MAHAN, in jungle fatigues and eyeblack, armed with an M16, Enters.)

ROGERS. Don't shoot! I'm an American! A friend! Amigo!

MAHAN. What in the holy bejeez 're you doing?

ROGERS. I'm down here on a due diligence trip. Gotta have a look-see before the loan gets approved. Had some time so ... What the hell 're you doing here?

MAHAN. Advising.

ROGERS. Advising who?

MAHAN. This your drive?

ROGERS. Second shot. No distance. All this humidity.

MAHAN. *(assessing ROGER'S next shot)* Whatcha usin'?

ROGERS. Nine iron.

MAHAN. Go with an eight.

End of Scene 3

Scene 4
The Other Economy

As LIGHTS come up we discover LANGLEY, in a bathrobe, with the front section of the New York Times in his hands. MAHAN lounges, sucking on a bottle of San Miguel, savoring his leisure.

LANGLEY. He was actually hiding behind his golf bag?

MAHAN. Yeah. ... I shoulda told him to go with a seven. The General 'll probably give him a medal for "Bravery on the Back Nine."

LANGLEY. And one to himself.

MAHAN. One more merit badge and the General better keep away from magnets. *(slight pause)* He's scheduled for perimeter control tonight. Oughta be a real circus. Old habits die hard. With any luck he'll make it through the night without shooting himself. Or me.

LANGLEY. *(looking up from the newspaper)* Interesting...

MAHAN. What?

LANGLEY. The General needs a fresh headline. Something that will give the red-baiters back home a minor hard-on. *(slight pause)* You remember the German? Used to work out of Marseilles and Cartegena.

MAHAN. Oh, *that* German. *(long pause)* I thought he was dead.

LANGLEY. He prefers it that way. We did brunch last Tuesday in Tegoose.

MAHAN. What's he selling *now?*

LANGLEY. The usual. Drugs, guns, scrubbed money. He just got his hands on an odd lot of Eastern bloc product. Small arms mostly.

MAHAN. What's the General need with more guns? He's already armed to the gills.

LANGLEY. But his opposition isn't. ... We'll buy the product on the coast. Bring it across the border at night. And then —

MAHAN. *(after a slight pause)* Ambush.

LANGLEY. How's that for a headline? ... Starting tomorrow, work the General's palace guard. See if they can pull this off without killing half the press corps.

MAHAN. Where they gonna get the money?

LANGLEY. The opposition?

MAHAN. Yeah.

(ROGERS appears in the doorway, drink in his hand.)

ROGERS. Hi, guys. ... Night-cap? *(A beat. LANGLEY and*

MAHAN look at one another.)

End of Scene 4

Scene 5
Rancho del Banco

In Blackout we hear the PANTING breath of a person, frightened and fleeing. Silence. Then a SCREAM. A low SPOTLITE sweeps the stage, joined by a second. Flicker of a human form. Then the LIGHTS sweep across a coiled length of shiny concertina wire stretched across the stage. The LIGHTS settle on a MAN, a peasant, hung up in the wire, assisted by a second peasant, a WOMAN. Pieces of firewood lie nearby.

MAN. *Ayyy! No jales tan recio! Vete! Escápate ahora. Yo me las averiguo. Anda. Escápate antes de que lleguen!* (Don't pull so hard. Go. Now. I'll be found. Run. Get out before they get here.)

(MAHAN Enters, leveling his M16 on the WOMAN. She freezes. NUEVA Enters. Strolls around her, then finally stops.)

NUEVA. Private property!!! *(slight pause)* This estate is private property!! You do not respect private property?!! Perhaps you do not believe in the *concept* of private property! Perhaps you are ... A COMMUNIST!!!

WOMAN. No.

NUEVA. *Quizás el es communista!* (Perhaps *he* is a communist!?)

WOMAN. *Esta finca era nuesta!* (This was our farm.) Farm. ... Mine.

NUEVA. *Esto es tierra de pastos.* Pasture land. *El Rancho del Banco!* The Ranch of the Bank!

WOMAN. *Necesitabamos leña.* (We needed firewood.)

NUEVA. *Para que?* (Why?)

WOMAN. *Para el fuego, señor.* (For fire, senor.)

MAHAN. What's she saying?

NUEVA. The rebels have been sabotaging the woods. Taking firewood. *(The MAN moans.)*

MAHAN. Hey, Indito! Shut up! You're freaking the friggin' cattle.

NUEVA. *Vienen aquí. Ignoran nuestros letreros.* (You come here. You ignore our signs.) They ignore our signs.

WOMAN. *No podemos leér, señor.* (We cannot read, senor.)

MAHAN. What's she saying?

NUEVA. The communists fill their ranks with illiterates.

WOMAN. *No somos comunistas! Bebemos Coca-Cola!* (We are not communist! We drink Coca Cola.)

MAHAN. What's that?

NUEVA. Coke.

MAHAN. Drugs?

NUEVA. Cola.

MAHAN. New, Diet, or Classic? *(MAHAN and NUEVA laugh. She does not understand. The MAN moans.)* Do something about him, willya? *(NUEVA shoots him. The WOMAN screams.)* Christ, you didn't have to kill him! He mighta been a friendly. He might have some intelligence. Ask her if she knows the wereabouts of them guerrillas.

NUEVA. *Los rebeles? Donde están?* (Where have the rebels gone?) *(NUEVA drags her away from the MAN, shoving her down over the wood.)* I think she knows. I think she is protecting them. ... Firewood, huh? ... Subversion. Theft. A defiance of property rights. A disrespect for the law, for the government, for my authority. Contempt! An insult! *(NUEVA turns his gun on the WOMAN.)*

MAHAN. *(stopping him from taking aim)* Don't do that! ... Tell her to get her firewood somewhere else. Tell her she can't come in here. Tell her this is a restricted zone. Let this be a warning. Tell her to spread the word.

NUEVA. They are spies for the subversives.

MAHAN. Tell her anyway. *(MAHAN Exits into the darkness. NUEVA waits a moment, watching him go. He starts to chamber another round in his revolver. The WOMAN attacks with a piece of firewood, knocking the gun out of NUEVA'S hand. They struggle. She grabs the gun and turns on him. He tries to talk her down.)*

NUEVA. *No, no, chica. To te pongas así.* (Now now, chica. Indita.) *(The WOMAN adopts a "shooter's" stance.) Dame la pistola. Anda. No te voy a hacer nada.* (Give it to me. Come now. I won't hurt you.) *(The WOMAN pulls the trigger. The safety is on.)*

MAHAN. *(off)* Yo! General! *(The WOMAN flees into the darkness with NUEVA'S gun. MAHAN Enters.)*

NUEVA. She won't be back. I scared her. She is no subversive. There are no subversives here. They are afraid to cross our frontier. They have disappeared into the hills, back across the border. *(noting NUEVA'S empty holster)*

MAHAN. Is that a fact?

NUEVA. Yes.

MAHAN. We're down here trying to help you get this situation under control, boy. You gotta strike fear into their hearts ... then show 'em a little mercy. That's how you win 'em over. Hearts and minds, son. Hearts and minds.

End of Scene 5

Scene 6
Yes, We Have Bananas

A Marketplace. Spread on the ground in front of the MAN and WOMAN are shawls and colorful dolls. Behind them, hat pulled low over his eyes, a shawl covering his shoulders is another man, the CADRE. We do not see his face.

MAN. *Mantas! Mantas y muñecas!* (Shawls! Shawls and dolls!)

WOMAN. *Muñecas! (Dolls!)*

MAN. *Mantas!* (Shawls!)

(The MAN spots ROGERS Entering, followed closely by LANGLEY and NUEVA. He shifts instantly to English.)

MAN. Shawls and dolls. Shawls and dolls. *(ROGERS approaches them.)*

WOMAN. Very nice. Big hit in United States. Craft fairs. Big bucks.

ROGERS. *(picking up one of the dolls)* Very nice.

MAN. Very nice. Big hit in United States. Big bucks.

WOMAN. Craft fairs. Authentic.

ROGERS. Now if they could mass produce these things...

MAN. Big bucks. Big hit in United States.

LANGLEY. They do.

ROGERS. But this is hand-crafted! *(NUEVA and LANGLEY exchange a look. ROGERS spots some bananas.)* What the hell are those?

LANGLEY. Bananas.

ROGERS. I can see that. But what are they doing here. Bananas are your major export crop. That and coffee and—

MAN. You want coffee?

ROGERS. The terms of your agreement with the IMF are to do something about your balance of payments problem. Now I want to know what the hell coffee and bananas are doing being sold here?! In the local market?! You're making it hard for me to bring back a good report. Very hard.

LANGLEY. Forget the bananas.

ROGERS. How can I? When they're right here?! In the open! Blatant!

LANGLEY. This is a market. They're capitalists. I'm telling you to forget the bananas.

ROGERS. No. *(NUEVA stomps off.)* This goes into my report. *(LANGLEY goes looking for the General. ROGERS waits until LANGLEY is gone before turning his attention to the peasants and their wares.)* How much? *(The WOMAN holds up four fingers.)* Four? *(The MAN holds up three fingers.)* Barter eh? I'll give you one. One! *Uno. (He holds up one finger. The WOMAN holds up one finger — her middle one.)* Very funny. Okay. I'll take five. Five! *(ROGERS holds up five fingers. The MAN hands him one doll and holds out his hand for payment.)* No! Five! For nine. Five for ... seven. *(They reject his offer. Off a subtle signal from the CADRE, the WOMAN offers ROGERS a shawl. She and the MAN put it around ROGER'S shoulders. She admires him in the shawl.)*

WOMAN. *Muy lindo!* (Very pretty!) *(ROGERS agrees. He then looks to the MAN who holds up ten fingers. ROGERS rejects the offer. A look is exchanged between the MAN and WOMAN. The WOMAN draws NUEVA'S chrome revolver from beneath her shawl and levels it at ROGERS.)*

ROGERS. Hey, now wait a minute here. I'm an American. You can't do that. I'm here to help you build an economy. Make it possible for you to sell for big bucks back in the states. *(The MAN flips the shawl over ROGERS' head, hooding him. The CADRE quickly ties ROGERS' hands behind his back. They take ROGERS away. The WOMAN settles back in behind her merchandise.)*

WOMAN. Shawls and dolls. Shawls and dolls.

(LANGLEY and NUEVA Re-enter.)

NUEVA. Where is he? Where'd he go? *(The WOMAN just stares at him.)* The man who was just here. Where is he? The American?

WOMAN. *(smiling, pointing to LANGLEY) Americano!*

NUEVA. (No! The other one? Where?)

WOMAN. *Desaparecio.* (Disappeared.) *(then to LANGLEY:)* Disappeared. *Muñeca?* (Doll?) *(NUEVA draws his gun. LANGLEY intervenes.)*

LANGLEY. You'd better go. I'll handle this.

NUEVA. We will be back, chica. *(NUEVA Exits. LANGLEY squats next to the WOMAN. He offers her a bill. She hands him a doll. He looks her in the eye then begins to count out about ten bills which she finally takes.)*

LANGLEY. Have your friend contact me at the Embassy. Identification code: "Expediency." You understand me? *(LANGLEY repeats his message in Spanish, then Exits. The WOMAN peels a banana, takes a bite. Smiles.)*

End of Scene 6

Scene 7
Name, Rank, and American Express Number

ROGERS, hooded with a kerchief, hands bound behind him, sits center stage surrounded by three guerrillas: the WOMAN, still armed with NUEVA'S chromeplated revolver; and the CADRE, who wears a bandolier of ammunition, an Ingram MAC-10 slung from his shoulder on a rope. The SOUND of HUEYS passing overhead continues.

ROGERS. What's that?

CADRE. Helicopters.

ROGERS. Yours or ours? *(Off a signal from the CADRE, the WOMAN smacks him soundly for his impertinence. ROGERS sprawls. She is about to pistol whip him but the CADRE signals her to desist.)* What do you want from me? Money Ransom? What?

CADRE. For now ... Information.

ROGERS. Whatever you want. Whatever I know. Could you take off this hood? Please? *(After a slight pause and a signal from the CADRE, the WOMAN kicks him. ROGERS begins kicking out wildly in all directions. The three guerrilas dance out of his way.)* FUCK YOU! You fuckin' grease-ball fucks! You're gonna have so many goddam U.S. Marines down here they'll be swarming up your assholes!!! *(The MAN smacks ROGERS' gut with the butt of his rifle. ROGERS moans. They haul him back up to a sitting position.)*

CADRE. Now ... Who sent you? *(ROGERS refuses to answer. The MAN grabs the hood, yanking back ROGERS head.)* Who sent you?

ROGERS. The bank. My bank. I work in a bank. I'm here to help. *(silence)* Your people and my people have a long-standing capital relationship. We're friends. Amigos! *(pause)* Say something dammit!

CADRE. Capital respects no borders. Neither do I. Borders are an imperialist fiction. Now who sent you?

ROGERS. My boss. At the bank.

CADRE. Not your government?

ROGERS. No. *(The MAN places the tip of the AK47 barrel against ROGER's ear.)* Not exactly.

CADRE. Ah. *(slight pause)* How? "Exactly"?

ROGERS. A man came to me. A briefing. From the government.

CADRE. His name?

ROGERS. I don't know. He uses different names.

CADRE. And what did he say?

ROGERS. Be nice to you people. Cut you some slack. Economically speaking.

CADRE. To strike a deal with one of your puppets?!! Isn't that right? *(another yank on the hood)*

ROGERS. Yes.

CADRE. And the money?

ROGERS. To repay the loans. I told you.

CADRE. You lend money so we can repay money we owe to you?

ROGERS. Happens all the time.

CADRE. What happens to the money?

ROGERS. Some's used for interest payments. Some's spent.

CADRE. And some is put into the private accounts of your puppets, deposited in your bank.

ROGERS. Maybe. *(The MAN yanks back ROGERS' head.)* Yes!!

CADRE. *La Bola.* (The ball.) *(The WOMAN slowly works her hand in ROGERS' pants pocket, much to the MAN'S amusement. She removes the golfball and tosses it to the CADRE who lifts the lower part of the hood, enough to expose ROGERS' mouth. The*

CADRE puts the golf ball into ROGERS' mouth. The MAN holds ROGERS' chin so that he cannot spit out the ball.) The man from your government is in our country isn't he? *(ROGERS nods his head "yes.")* At the Hotel International. *(ROGERS nods his head "yes.")* Just like you. *(ROGERS nods "yes.")* I think you too are from your government. *(ROGERS shakes his head "no.")* Si. Si. Si. ... C-I-A. *(ROGERS shakes his head "no." A desperate denial. The CADRE pulls the hood back down over ROGERS' mouth. ROGERS cannot spit out the golf ball. He is choking. The sound of CHOPPERS returns. The MAN kicks ROGERS over. The CADRE Exits.)*

End of Scene 7

Scene 8
Double Espresso

MAHAN and NUEVA sit opposite one another on ammunition crates — or bags — both holding demitasses filled with espresso. The sound of CHOPPERS continues overhead. LANGLEY stands slightly upstage from them, noticeably disengaged from the round of toasts.

MAHAN. To war.
NUEVA. The good life. Rape, plunder...
MAHAN. ...and "humanitarian" aid.
NUEVA. Especially rape. ... It is so difficult to motivate

the troops. There are so few chickens for them to steal. Fortunately the young women are ... *(NUEVA and MAHAN share a lewd laugh.)*

MAHAN. I love a good war. It's been a while. May you populate your country with anti-communists. *(NUEVA laughs. THEY toast again.)*

LANGLEY. The shipment of Cuban arms arrived this morning. I've arranged for the trucks to cross the border tonight. Are your people ready to intercept?

NUEVA. Of course. And the journalists?

LANGLEY. They'll be there. *Time,* AP, UPI. Two bureau chiefs and a stringer.

NUEVA. *Excellente.* So ... where did you get the weapons? *(when LANGLEY doesn't answer)* Black market? ... Expensive?

LANGLEY. You're not paying for them, are you?

NUEVA. *(after a slight pause)* And the banker?

LANGLEY. Ah, the Banker. With any luck they'll negotiate for his release. Better publicity that way.

NUEVA. What if they kill him?

LANGLEY. Makes it harder to build a case but we can handle it.

NUEVA. But what if his bosses take this as a sign of instability?

LANGLEY. *(smiling)* Just the opposite, friend. *(Exits.)*

NUEVA. I don't understand.

MAHAN. *You're* going to free him.

(LANGLEY returns with the CADRE who has just handed him a map.)

CADRE. The location is marked. *(The CADRE and NUEVA are both shocked to see one another. They stare at one another, hands on their pistols.)*

LANGLEY. You didn't hurt him did you?

CADRE. A few bruises.

LANGLEY. Fine. *(Off a signal from LANGLEY, MAHAN holds up a canvas bag filled with money. The CADRE is forced to cross in front of NUEVA to accept his payment. He checks the contents, then Exits. LANGLEY hands the map to NUEVA.)* Send someone out to pick up the banker. Take him to a safe house and hold him.

NUEVA. Isn't he...

LANGLEY. The enemy.

MAHAN. Can't have a war without an enemy.

LANGLEY. Or an enemy without weapons.

MAHAN. Nice thing about these Low-Intensity Conflicts is they draw heat off the home fires. Start sending 18-year-olds off to get their noogies whacked in places their girlfriends can't pronounce and you got hell to pay at the ballot box.

LANGLEY. Opposition and dissent are only good for one thing...

NUEVA. Target practice.

MAHAN. *(greatly amused)* Listen to this guy, willya? *(MAHAN ushers NUEVA back to his seat.)* Like the old Mafioso used to say: Keep your friends close...

LANGLEY. And your enemies closer.

NUEVA. Ah. *(when his grin disappears, to LANGLEY:)* You're a real son of a bitch.

MAHAN. Yeah. ... But at least he's *your* son of a bitch. *(LANGLEY finally toasts NUEVA with a demitasse.)*

LANGLEY. To ... The "Expedient." *(NUEVA returns the toast.)*

End of Scene 8

Scene 9
Behind the "Veil"

Upstage, a thicket of brush. ROGERS, still hooded, hands tied behind him, sits center stage. MAHAN, armed, Enters cautiously, checks the perimeter in silence. ROGERS senses his presence. Alert. He follows the sounds with his head. All secure, NUEVA Enters. MAHAN Exits. NUEVA approaches ROGERS. ROGERS freezes. NUEVA cuts his bonds. ROGERS raises his hands in surrender. NUEVA pulls up the hood, catching the golfball when ROGERS spits it out.

ROGERS. It's you!

NUEVA. I *personally* negotiated for your release. These people are savages. But also greedy.

ROGERS. I thought they were going to kill me.

NUEVA. I swear to you, when we catch them, I will let you kill them yourself.

(Rumble of a TRUCK approaching.)

ROGERS. *(frightened)* What's that?

NUEVA. Trucks. Enemy weapons. ... Listen.

(They do. Finally, GUNFIRE erupts. A firefight in the near distance.)

ROGERS. What's that?

NUEVA. We have intercepted their shipment. *(pause)* You'll read all about it in *Time* magazine. The communists cannot win. Come. *(The GUNFIRE fades.)*

ROGERS. Where are we going?

NUEVA. To a safe place.

ROGERS. Forget it. I've seen enough. I'm going home.

NUEVA. In due time.

(The barrel of a rifle — or AK47 — slowly pushes out from the brush, aimed at NUEVA, and incidentally at ROGERS.)

ROGERS. I'll give a good report. You'll get your loans.

(Suddenly, MAHAN rises up behind the bush, garroting a masked MAN. The rifle drops. MAHAN finishes the job. ROGERS and NUEVA are shocked. MAHAN lets the dead man drop, picks up his weapon then approaches NUEVA and ROGERS.)

NUEVA. How could you let this happen?!!

MAHAN. Hey, pal, I just saved your butt.

NUEVA. If you keep my enemies any closer, I'll be dead!! *(Exits.)*

MAHAN. *(re: the rifle)* It's Cuban.

ROGERS. Didn't he pay them for my release?

MAHAN. One hundred thousand. And that's in U.S. dollars, friend.

ROGERS. But they would have killed me anyway?

(MAHAN shrugs, then pushes the confiscated gun into ROGERS' hands. A comradely blow to ROGERS' shoulder, then MAHAN Exits, leaving ROGERS alone in the dark, with the dead man, with GUNFIRE in the distance.)

End of Scene 9

Scene 10
Drinks on the House

ROGERS is at a cafe table with the WOMAN, now dressed in her sexiest garb, a convincing portrait of a B-girl. The MAN waits on the tables. ROGERS finishes another gulp of his drink.

ROGERS. So there I was, surrounded by these guys, enough hardware to take down a convoy, and this one faggot comes in at me — I still got my hands tied behind me, see — and I give him a kick in the balls hard enough to cut the next six limbs off his family tree. *Bolas! (ROGERS demonstrates his kick, complete with sound effects before continuing. The WOMAN stares at him.)* Well he starts screaming and crying and his men see what a wimp he is, so then, *then* he leans his ugly face in close to mine, trying to wilt me with his lousy breath, and I bit his goddam nose.

WOMAN. Muy macho. *(The WOMAN strokes and caresses ROGERS' bicep feigning admiration for his strength. He signals the waiter for another round of drinks.)*

ROGERS. They had themselves a tiger by the tail, let me tell you. You hear these stories about hostages rolling over, wimping out. Not me. *(The MAN returns with their drinks then waits for payment.)* If I didn't have to get back to the States, I'd go get'em myself. But... I gotta unwind. Y' know what I mean? Last night. Gotta make the most of it. What I need is a party. A private party. *(He winks at her. She smiles. He leers. She licks her lips and strokes his leg.)* Yeah. *(ROGERS senses then MAN'S presence at his shoulder, hands him some coins.)* Keep the change, Juan.

(Latin juke box MUSIC comes up. A Latin covered, American pop tune.)

ROGERS. I love that song! *(The WOMAN leads him into a dance. He twirls her into a samba, dancing. She laughs and dances with him. He tries to kiss her. Misses. Tries to paw her. She squirms free motioning him to hold back. She flashes her skirts. He leers. She opens her large pocketbook and slowly, suggestively, pulls out an exotic piece of lingerie.)* Oh yes! Yes!! *(She smiles, licks her lips again, flashes some thigh, then with a wink she reaches into her bag again.)* Another surprise for me?

WOMAN. *Si.*

(The MUSIC stops dead. A pulled plug. The WOMAN pulls out

the chrome-plated sidearm and trains it on ROGERS.)

ROGERS. What the hell is this? *(ROGERS assumes that this is a simple Murphy-scene robbery. He hands his wallet over to the MAN, who seems puzzled by ROGERS' action. Now ROGERS is confused.)* So what is it you want?

MAN. Answers.

WOMAN. Your ransom?

MAN. Who took the money? ... Who took the money?!

ROGERS. A man.

WOMAN. What man?

ROGERS. A man. Men. I don't know. *(She levels the gun at his face.)* Revolutionaries!!

MAN. How much?

WOMAN. *(training the gun on his "bolas")* How much?!

ROGERS. *(highly articulated)* One hundred thousand.

(The MAN and WOMAN look at one another. Beat. The MAN strokes ROGERS shoulders to relax him then leans in close on ROGERS' face breathing hard on him. ROGERS squirms. The MAN bites ROGERS' nose. ROGERS howls and screams, covering his face with his hands. LIGHTS out. ROGERS keeps howling.)

End of Scene 10

Scene 11
Spoils of War

The CADRE, by guttering candlelight, counts out a huge pile of American currency. We may hear covering dialogue of the MAN and WOMAN.

MAN. *(off) Vamos! Corre! Apúrate! Hay que decírselo!*

(The MAN and WOMAN, armed, Enter.)

MAN. *(re: the money) Qué haces?* (What's this?)

CADRE. *Contando el dinero. Para las armas.* (Counting the money. For the arms.) Ransom. *Para el banquero.* (For the Banker.) *(They don't believe him. The MAN and WOMAN level their guns on the CADRE.)*

MAN. *Eres un traidor.* (You're a traitor.)

CADRE. *Nunca!* (Never!) *Este dinero es para las armas. Sin armas no hay revolución y si so hay dinero no hay armas!* (This money is for arms! No money, no arms. No arms, no revolution!)

WOMAN. *Te vimos con el americano.* (We saw you with the American.)

MAN. *Sí.*

CADRE. *(holding up fistfuls of money) SI! Cambiándolo por esto.* (Exchanging him for this!)

MAN. *Por cuánto?!* (How much?)

CADRE. *Ocheinticinco mil dólares norteamericanos!* (Eighty-five thousand dollars.) *Véanlo. Ahí está todo.* (See, it's all here!) *(The WOMAN holds the candle up to the CADRE'S face. She studies him.)*

WOMAN. *Si el dinero era para las armas, por qué todavía tienes el dinero aquí?* (If the money is for arms, why's the money still here?)

CADRE. *Iba a pagar noche.* (I was to pay tonight.) Tonight. *Despues del "delivery."* (After "delivery.") *No hubo "delivery." Por eso todavia tengo el dinero.* (The delivery was not made. I still have the money.)

WOMAN. *Se llevaron las armas.* (The arms were taken.)

CADRE. *QUE?!!* (WHAT?!!)

MAN. *En una emboscada!* (In an ambush.)

CADRE. *(shocked)* Ambush.

WOMAN. *Lo sabían.* (They knew.)

MAN. *Tu se lo informaste. Has traicionado a la revolución!* (You told them. You betrayed the revolution.)

CADRE. No. *Nunca!* Never! *(Off a signal from the WOMAN who holds the candle close to the CADRE, the MAN searches inside the CADRE'S coat for the missing $15,000. He finds it.)*

MAN. *Para* "information"?

CADRE. *(angrily snatching it back) Gastos.* (Expenses.) *(He uses the candle to light a cigarette.)* Expenses. *(He blows out the candle.)*

End of Scene 11

Scene 12
Southern Air Transport

Sound of a prop PLANE taking off. ROGERS rushes on with his suitcase, golfbag, and suit coat, an airline ticket envelope sticking out of his shirt pocket, a large white adhesive bandage on his nose. He sits on his upended suitcase, his golf bag at his feet. The sun is hot, brutal. He wipes his neck and face with a soiled handkerchief. When he accidentally brushes his nose, he yelps in pain.

Two PEASANTS, the MAN and the WOMAN, Enter, carrying what appear to be large sacks of coffee. They drop the bags nearby and squat. They stare at ROGERS, ROGERS stares back.

ROGERS. You waiting for the plane? *(The PEASANTS stare at him blankly.)* Aeroplane?! *(ROGERS tries to pantomime an airplane in flight, complete with sound effects. The PEASANTS just stare vacantly.)* What time? What time airplane come land? *(ROGERS keeps pointing at his watch. The MAN scratches himself. The WOMAN breaks wind. No change in their expressions. ROGERS sits back down on his suitcase. Each time he glances over at them, he encounters their vacant stares. He wipes his brow.)* Hot. ... Helluva day to be lugging that stuff around, huh? *(ROGERS rises, checks the sky again, then approaches the PEASANTS.)* Hey, I'm not interested in taking anything from you. I'm an American. See. *(ROGERS takes out a dollar bill and shows it to them.)* American!

Americano! That's George Washington. Father of our country. Winner of our *revolución.* Our *Bola.* I'd show you Lincoln and Jackson, but one of your buddies stole my wallet. *(slight pause)* You don't have the foggiest idea what I'm talking about, do you? *(No response at all from the PEASANTS. ROGERS puts on his biggest friendliest smile.)*

(The CADRE Enters quietly behind him.)

ROGERS. You know what I think of your shitpile of a backwater piece of dirt country? I think you should all get the trots so bad you wash yourselves right into the fucking ocean! *(Suddenly, the PEASANTS jump to their feet. ROGERS backs off a pace or two, nervously.)* Oh shit, they speak English.

CADRE. At least they do not speak like Richard Fucking Nixon. *(The CADRE goes to the peasants and pays them each a few bills.)* I couldn't help but overhear your speech.

ROGERS. *(suddenly terrified when the CADRE opens his fatigue jacket revealing the fact that he is heavily armed)* I was just playing a little joke on 'em. Passing time til the plane comes. I didn't *mean* all that.

CADRE. The plane?

ROGERS. You too? *(The CADRE says nothing but studies ROGERS closely. ROGERS shows the CADRE his ticket.)* I had to trade a First Class ticket on Pan Am for this! You ever hear of this airline?

CADRE. You are my contact?

ROGERS. For what?

CADRE. *(pointing to the PEASANTS' bags)* That! *(then with a chuckle) You* are the money man? *(ROGERS beams, taking this as a compliment.)* And I thought ... Well, never mind. *(indicating ROGERS' bag)* Is it in there?

ROGERS. *(moving protectively in front of his luggage — very much like the PEASANTS did to protect their bags)* What's in what?

CADRE. The money! The two hundred thousand dollars!

ROGERS. You people kidnapped me once. You got what you wanted. Once is enough.

CADRE. *(dangerously)* Just give me the bag.

ROGERS. *(grabbing his suitcase and retreating)* No! This is part of a matched set!

(The SOUND of an approaching airplane. LANGLEY Enters with an attaché case. ROGERS and the CADRE are so preoccupied with one another and the plane's arrival, only the two PEASANTS notice LANGLEY's arrival. LANGLEY steps between them, handing the attaché case to the CADRE.)

LANGLEY. It's all there.

CADRE. So if he's not—

LANGLEY. He's just the banker.

CADRE. Ah. *El Banquero! (LANGLEY goes to the bags to check the contents. He pulls out a kilo bag of white powder. The CADRE offers ROGERS his hand and shakes it vigorously.)* International finance has always been one of my many ... interests. We should talk sometime.

LANGLEY. *(to the CADRE:)* Now beat it. *(ROGERS starts to Exit toward the waiting prop plane with his luggage.)* Not you! *(ROGERS stops momentarily. The CADRE laughs. LANGLEY shoots a look at the CADRE who starts to Exit. LANGLEY sends the PEASANTS off toward the plane. ROGERS begins to follow them.)*

LANGLEY. Where the hell do you think you're going now?

ROGERS. Getting on the plane.

LANGLEY. You weren't supposed to be here.

ROGERS. Do you know how many frequent flier miles I lost just to get on that flight?!

LANGLEY. There are other airlines. *(As soon as LANGLEY turns to go, ROGERS lifts his bags, starting for the plane.)* I'll charter a friggin' jet!! *(ROGERS stares longingly off in the direction of the PLANE which, judging from the sounds, is beginning its take-off.)* That plane will be busted by the D.E.A. when it lands. Now come on.

(They start to go. The plane is in the air and then suddenly it EXPLODES. SOUND and flash of LIGHT. ROGERS is dumbfounded. LANGLEY is shocked. The CADRE Re-enters, grinning. ROGERS looks to LANGLEY for some explanation. LANGLEY doesn't have one. ROGERS assumes that LANGLEY had something to do with the plane's destruction.)

ROGERS. You mean, you...?

CADRE. *(stepping forward in defense of LANGLEY, who eyes the CADRE with growing suspicion)* Noooo. How could this man *(LANGLEY)* condone, let alone participate in any kind of terrorist activity or the importation of contraband? *(to LANGLEY:)* Or *ambush?*... Impossible. Absurd. Correct? *(The CADRE just stares at LANGLEY who can neither affirm nor deny. ROGERS watches the flaming remnants of the crash.)*

ROGERS. Guess this means coca's down again, huh?

End of Scene 12

Scene 13
After the Ball

LANGLEY sits in the dark. His back to the audience. He lights a cigarette. Offstage, we hear NUEVA singing, slightly drunk, coming home. He Enters. Stops.

NUEVA. Who's there?

LANGLEY. *(after a slight pause)* How was the party?

NUEVA. It's you. Thank God. I thought ... Let me turn on a light.

LANGLEY. No.

NUEVA. *(remaining just inside the backlit doorway)* The reception was magnificent. Your Ambassador is an extraordinary host. All the most important people were there. I saw Senor and Senora—

LANGLEY. You have an interesting little chat with the Cultural Attaché? ... Tall guy. Blond. Good-looking. Armani suit.

NUEVA. Yes. Charming young man.

LANGLEY. I know.

NUEVA. We talked about baseball. Nicaraguan infielders; Costa Rican pitchers; the Cubans. In my youth I was a slugger. .310 one year in the Army League. I played shortstop.

LANGLEY. I'm sure you were quite the playmaker.

NUEVA. I don't understand why you never go to these parties.

LANGLEY. Technically, friend, I'm in Argentina. On vacation. I left yesterday, remember? But let's get back to those Cubans. Specifically, those Cuban-crated, Czech-made, standard-issue infantry assault weapons? Weapons which were to have been warehoused? Weapons which, miracle of miracles, recently arrived in—

NUEVA. *(taking offense)* If you are suggesting that I—

LANGLEY. They don't work. *(slight pause)* The rifles don't work. They're rigged. Booby-trapped! On full automatic they explode.

NUEVA. *Oh Madre de Dios.*

LANGLEY. A little precaution I took — just in case your crack special forces unit took the wrong map, the wrong trail or the wrong trucks and the weapons ended up in the hands of your opposition.

NUEVA. Why didn't you tell me?

LANGLEY. I didn't think that you would re-sell them. I especially did not think that you would be stupid enough to sell them to a supposed ally! Without asking.

NUEVA. They needed arms. Desperately. Your Congress gives them nothing. If your politicians would take their heads out of their asses—

LANGLEY. *(to his feet, face to face with NUEVA)* You'd better hope you stashed that money somewhere down a paper-trail so thick the light never finds it. You've got a loose tongue, Senor General. A dangerous trait for a man in your tenuous position. *(slight pause)* You see, that nice handsome clean-cut cultural attaché posts me memos. Unfortunately, he also routes them through the Director of Operations who's got a penchant for covering his politically sensitive ass. He'll cover his by exposing mine. Until now, I've had a profound interest in making you look better than you deserve. Keep that cash very liquid, my friend. You may need it.

NUEVA. Why?

LANGLEY. Travel expenses. *(Exits.)*

End of Scene 13

Scene 14
P.S., Send Fresh Underwear

The MAN is seated at a Telex machine or its equivalent. ROGERS is dictating a report to the home office. His nose is still bandaged.

ROGERS. Even with Coca — that's "*Coca*" — down, the present regime seems amenable to — strike that — uh ... *(He looks over the MAN'S shoulder at the text.)* Not "amenable to strikes", you idiot!! Delete it. ... The whole thing! No! Get rid of "the present regime" there — Don't type *that* for Chrissakes!! Move over. *(ROGERS ushers the MAN aside and sits down in front of the machine. He types, hunting and pecking. The MAN looks over his shoulder. ROGERS, feeling the eyes, tries to hide the content with his body. ROGERS turns accusingly on the MAN. The MAN backs off slightly. ROGERS goes back to work, making an error, blaming it on the machine.)* Doesn't *anything* work in this lousy country?! *(ROGERS resumes typing.)*

(The CADRE Enters, armed with his MAC-10 machine pistol. He signals the MAN to leave. The MAN does.)

CADRE. *(very friendly) Buenas noches.*

ROGERS. *(Leaps to his feet, throws up his hands in surrender. The CADRE just smiles at him. ROGERS offers him all the money in his pocket. The CADRE laughs.)* What do you want?

CADRE. Conversation. One intelligent man to another. Two "Americans" — North, South. *(slight pause)* We've met before, you know.

ROGERS. That little scene out at the airfield—

CADRE. Twenty years ago. ... You shot a seventy-nine.

ROGERS. *(testing the waters)* With a double-bogey—

CADRE. On the fifteenth. I was your caddy.

ROGERS. No shit?!!

CADRE. I was very impressed. Also very young.

ROGERS. Small fucking world, huh?

CADRE. And here we are.

ROGERS. And here we are.

CADRE. We've both come a long way. You into the highest echelons of finance, and me, well ... I'm still struggling. My English was very poor. So was my family.

ROGERS. Helluvan improvement if you don't mind my saying so. Your English, I mean.

CADRE. Reading. *The Financial Times, Wall Street Journal.*

ROGERS. And Marx.

CADRE. Of course. *(The CADRE then sidles over to the Telex machine, leaning past ROGERS who tries to block his view.)* So this is your report?

ROGERS. Part of it. ... Why? ... You don't like it? *(pause)* Something missing?

CADRE. A few things.

ROGERS. Such as?

CADRE. The General.

ROGERS. Oh. Him.

CADRE. You don't like him? *(ROGERS doesn't answer.)* An unsrupulous man.

ROGERS. And you?

CADRE. I take the long-view. Perhaps that makes me an idealist. Perhaps my ideals make me dangerous. To men like you. But especially to men like him.

ROGERS. Do things different if you were in power, would you?

CADRE. Oh, si, senor. Very differently.

ROGERS. *(cagily, after a pause)* What's your chances?

CADRE. Of?

ROGERS. Power.

CADRE. Depends.

ROGERS. On?

CADRE. Your government. Your bank. My intelligence and perseverance. ... Your general's avarice.

ROGERS. He's not "my" general.

CADRE. *(pounding the machine for emphasis)* Nor mine. See, already we agree on so many things. *(slight pause)* I would hate to see my people fall deeper into debt simply to enrich a foolish man. When he is gone, his obligations will remain.

ROGERS. *(after a pause)* If— and I'm only saying "If" — you succeeded him, you'd honor those obligations.

CADRE. What do you think?

ROGERS. I think you'd have to.

CADRE. I do whatever I have to do.

ROGERS. *(after another pause)* I see.

CADRE. I think you do. Have a pleasant journey home, amigo. *(The CADRE shakes ROGERS' hand.)*

ROGERS. Thank you. *(The CADRE begins to Exit.)* Uh, by the way ... did I tip you?

CADRE. As your caddy?

ROGERS. Yes.

CADRE. No.

End of Scene 14

Scene 15
Marionettes

MAHAN holds a sheaf of standard computer print-out.

LANGLEY opens a top-secret pouch. He removes the contents then hands the envelope to MAHAN and who reads the blue-bordered cover while LANGLEY reads the directive.

MAHAN. Jesus. "Top Secret; Eyes Only; Sensitive; Action; with an UMBRA, NOFORN, NONCONTRACT, PROPIN, *and* an ORCON. God ain't cleared high enough for this! Who do they want us to nuke? *(LANGLEY hands him an 8x10 glossy of NUEVA.)* Oh man, the General. ... You groom this guy for three years, crease the pants on the business suits, lay the pipes, and the minute you get the conduits gushing, whaddaya get?...

LANGLEY. "Reprioritization."

MAHAN. It had to have been written by that tweedy little twit at the Foundation.

LANGLEY. Never had the pleasure.

MAHAN. Consider yourself lucky.

LANGLEY. Still ... *(A wicked smile creeps onto LANGLEY'S face. MAHAN is all ears.)* Interesting. *(LANGLEY continues studying the dispatch. MAHAN is beside himself with curiosity. Finally, he can't wait any longer.)*

MAHAN. C'mon, man, you gotta give me something.

LANGLEY. When you need to know, I'll let you know.

MAHAN. *(disappointed)* Yes, sir. *(MAHAN takes another long look at the photo of NUEVA. Very serious.)* When?

LANGLEY. Maybe never. Like this conversation. It maybe never happened. *(After a slight pause, LANGLEY hands MAHAN an 8x10 of the CADRE.)*

MAHAN. The new horse? *(after a moment's consideration)* Manageable.

LANGLEY. Barely. "A history of absolute unmitigated hostility toward our interests." a pragmatist, he understands the value in swapping fine print with the devil. He'll be *unmanageable,* but predictable. Within limits. He'll believe he can use us because he believes he can outsmart us. We'll encourage that particular delusion.

MAHAN. *(opening the computer print-out copies of ROGERS' telexes for LANGLEY)* Now, about the banker...

LANGLEY. *(scanning them)* If this is their idea of "due diligence," no wonder the banks are cracking.

MAHAN. *(pointing out a passage)* No way that clown *ever* broke eighty! I don't care if he had Che fuckin' Guevara for a caddy!

LANGLEY. Oh hell, why wait? Send him in.

(MAHAN Exits and returns with ROGERS, his nose still prominently bandaged, his suit a mess. LANGLEY turns on the warmth and gives ROGERS a friendly solicitous greeting.)

LANGLEY. How's the nose?

ROGERS. Terrible. I think it's infected. God knows what diseases these people carry!

LANGLEY. *(to MAHAN:)* Make sure our friend gets whatever attention he needs. Arrange it with our chief physician. *(MAHAN Exits.)*

ROGERS. I'd rather go home.

LANGLEY. You'll love this guy. He's the best in the region. I'd trust him with my life. Or my nose.

ROGERS. When can I leave?

LANGLEY. Soon.

ROGERS. I've seen all I need to see. They'll get their money. Not because they deserve it—

LANGLEY. Exactly.

ROGERS. But because — How's that?

LANGLEY. They don't deserve it. And you shouldn't approve the new disbursement *or* the rescheduling.

ROGERS. But I thought—

LANGLEY. Yes, yes, I know. We made a mistake. *(Slaps himself on the wrist.)* An honest one, but still ... New information has recently come to our attention which suggests major instability.

ROGERS. Meaning?

LANGLEY. A coup.

ROGERS. A coup?!

LANGLEY. Asia has its monsoons, Central America its coups. We trust that the new regime, while superficially less synchronistic with your own agenda, will prove far more reliable. In the long haul. And given the size of the debt, that should be our chief concern. Don't you agree?

ROGERS. Well, yes. This new regime—

LANGLEY. *(showing ROGERS the picture of CADRE)* I believe you already know the man.

ROGERS. That man is a rebel! And a drug dealer!!!

LANGLEY. If you'll recall, in that particular incident, I too could be identified as a drug dealer. He's also the man who negotiated for your release and, quite frankly, the man who saved your life.

ROGERS. I thought the General—

LANGLEY. This man never actually laid a hand on you, did he?

ROGERS. I'm not sure. I couldn't see who—

LANGLEY. *(overriding)* He didn't. I assure you. *(LANGLEY hands ROGERS the copies of his telexes, pointing out select passages.)* Hell, if it weren't for your "favorable" comments on him ... well...

ROGERS. *(scanning the telex text)* Oh, I never meant...

LANGLEY. Of course not. ... Must've been a helluva caddy.

ROGERS. What makes you say that?

LANGLEY. *(pointing out the incriminating relevant passage in one of the telexes)* A fifty dollar tip's better than okay. *(He takes the telexes from ROGERS.)* I'm overstepping my bounds by telling you any of this. This information is of the absolutely highest confideniality. I am in complete violation of national security. I could be busted to a desk in Virginia, probably court-martialed, possibly convicted. But I felt that, having brought you here and after what you've been through — between being kidnapped and ... bitten — the least I could do was share this information with you. A meeting's being arranged. But first, let's get you to a doctor.

ROGERS. Thank you. I appreciate it.

LANGLEY. You owe me one.

End of Scene 15

Scene 16
Nocturnal Visitors

In faint MOONLIGHT, the CADRE, the MAN, and the WOMAN, are bivouaced for the night. The MAN is on the edge of sleep. The WOMAN massages the CADRE'S shoulders. Night SOUNDS. A shadowy, armed and masked FIGURE moves silently upstage from them.

CADRE. *Que tiempos estos. Me persigue el gobierno como si yo fuera un chihuahua. Me molestan los gringos. Y hasta alguno de los compan¡eros sospechan de mi. Y todo por un poco de dinero.* (Such times. ... Hunted by the government like a "dog." Harassed by the Gringos. Suspected by my own people— for a few dollars...)

(Suddenly, TWO MEN, both darkly dressed, both wearing masks, move on the GUERRILLAS. LANGLEY takes the WOMAN from behind, a knife to her throat. MAHAN'S gun is in the CADRE'S face.)

MAHAN. *(in a harsh whisper to the MAN)* Lay down your weapons. ... Now! *(He does. LANGLEY finds the chrome plated pistol on the WOMAN and takes it. MAHAN, to the CADRE:)* You! With us! *(The CADRE is taken away, the WOMAN released. The MAN and WOMAN are about to flee when they hear the COCK of weapons. They freeze, hands up.)*

End of Scene 16

Scene 17
Confiteor Omne Peccata Mea

A SCREAM in the dark. As LIGHTS come up we discover the WOMAN is strapped to the bare metal box springs of a bed. The MAN, his hands bound behind him, slumped to his knees, is forced to watch. NUEVA interrogates.

NUEVA. I am a reasonable man. I have no heart for such things. *Pero tu líder ha desaparecido y tengo que saber donde y por qué.* (Your leader has disappeared. I need to know where he's gone and why.) *(The WOMAN spits at him.) Dónde está?* (Where is he?)

WOMAN. *No le decimos nada!* (We say nothing to you!) *(Off a signal from NUEVA, ELECTRICITY surges through the metal springs. The WOMAN convulses. The MAN tries to look away. NUEVA holds his head toward the bed.)*

NUEVA. *Mírala! MIRALA!* (Look at her! LOOK AT HER!) ... Stop! *(The voltage stops. The aftershocks twitch through the WOMAN'S extremities. She finally grows still.) No puede más. Cómo dejas que tu mujer sufra así? No eres hombre? Otra descarga como la última y se muere. Ni a tí te reconocerá. Puedes salvarla dándome unas simples respuestas. Vamos. Dónde está? DONDE?!! Otra vez!!* (She cannot take much more. ... How can you stand to see your woman suffer so? Are you not a man? A few more like the last one and she will die and if not, her brain will be dead ... She will not even recognize you. You can save her by giving me a few simple answers. Now where is he? WHERE? ... Again!)

MAN. NO!!!

NUEVA. *Otre vez!* (Again!)

MAN. No! *(NUEVA moves closer to the MAN, leaning down to hear him.) Americanos.*

NUEVA. *Americanos. ¿Cómo lo sabes?* (Americans? How do you know?)

MAN. *Los oí. Por el acento. La peste. Estaba muy oscura para verlos. Por favor. Se lo juro que eran americanos. Lo juro. Por favor, no le haga más daño...* (I heard them. Their accents. Their smell. It was too dark to see. I swear to you they were Americans. I swear. Please...) *(NUEVA regards him for a long moment, then cuts his bonds free. The MAN goes to the WOMAN. She is dead. The MAN turns to NUEVA then slowly approaches him.) Maldito seas.* (Damn you.) *(The MAN lunges for NUEVA'S throat. In reflex he raises the knife. The MAN impales himself on the point. The MAN falls to the floor, clutching his belly. He dies. NUEVA removes the knife. He regards the dead MAN and WOMAN while wiping the blade clean.)*

NUEVA. Dispose of them. *(NUEVA "crosses" himself in Catholic contrition, then Exits.)*

End of Scene 17

Scene 18
The Big Picture

MAHAN leads the CADRE, blindfolded and hands tied behind his back, into a room which is empty except for two chairs. MAHAN puts him into a chair then removes the blindfold.

CADRE. Where am I?

MAHAN. We got this little place back home we call "shit creek." You maybe heard of it. Well, son, I'd put you about six miles downstream, heading for the falls. And the one thing you gotta be wondering right about now is whether you got a paddle. *(slight pause)* I figure you for one of them "big picture" guys.

CADRE. Like your boss.

MAHAN. I ain't thought much about it till just now. But I'd say — and this's just one simple country boy's take on it — but I'd say, your "big picture" ain't but a teensy piece of his "picture," a little splotch down in the corner of his giant jigsaw. Maybe you fit, maybe you don't. But you sure as hell better hope you do.

CADRE. And if I don't?

MAHAN. *(deftly drawing his knife from his boot and placing the edge against the CADRE'S throat)* He gets me to cut off the edges.

CADRE. And you always do what you're told.

MAHAN. I'm real good at following orders. My heart is pure, my mind is clear.

CADRE. Your mind is...

MAHAN. What?

CADRE. *No importa.* (Never mind.)

MAHAN. Where you got it all wrong is thinking I got a problem with not dealing with the "big picture." Now the little things, I pay real close attention to. Most times I get but one shot. One mistake and that's all she wrote.

CADRE. Shit cheek and no paddle.

MAHAN. See! Now you got it. *(Sits next to the CADRE. Pause.)* So how'd you pop the plane?

CADRE. Maybe I didn't.

MAHAN. Fuck "deniability," Josë, I'm just interested in technique. The bags musta been the plant but the plane blew too low for an altitude switch. Coulda been a radio control but an inside job with one of your men—

CADRE. Or women. Revolution is an equal opportunity employer. *(The CADRE smiles. MAHAN smiles. Long pause. MAHAN "gets" it.)*

MAHAN. "Gravity switch!!!" A couple G's and BOOM! Nice. Very nice. Pretty fuckin' sophisticated, though.

CADRE. We are not all poor peasants, you know. Some of us even studied at your American universities and then came home.

MAHAN. Why?

CADRE. This is their home.

MAHAN. No. I mean, why'd you blow the plane?

CADRE. You *are* a simple man, aren't you?

MAHAN. Stompin' in the snake pit. Just like you.

CADRE. Ah, but I am home and you are very far away.

MAHAN. "Home" is where I pouch my postcards to. The "bush" is *my* habitat.

CADRE. Even when the bush is mine?

MAHAN. Not yet it ain't.

CADRE. Soon.

MAHAN. "Soon" may be a long time comin'. Maybe

not even in your lifetime.

CADRE. Or yours.

MAHAN. *(after a pause)* Now there is a way "soon" could come sooner than later.

CADRE. Ah.

MAHAN. Any time now the Man's gonna come through that door to have a little talk with you.

CADRE. About the General's future?

MAHAN. The Man's preparing him a little political IQ test — see if the General's got what it takes. You better hope he don't.

CADRE. The General ... The General is one of those pathetic little men, lost in the middle — hungry enough to kiss the hand but not enough to bite it! *(slight pause)* Does your boss expect me to take the same IQ test?

MAHAN. *(Draws his knife again. The CADRE tenses. MAHAN cuts the CADRE loose. The CADRE rubs his hands.)* I'd hear him out. Listen real close to what he's got to say. *(slight pause)* Play it real tight. Try bluffing and he'll wipe the table with your butt. *(Exits.)*

End of Scene 18

Scene 19
Let's Make a Deal

The CADRE sits silently while LANGLEY stands nearby. Pause.

LANGLEY. Well?

CADRE. Never. *Nunca!* Never!!

LANGLEY. "Never" is a very long time, my friend.

CADRE. I am *not* your friend.

LANGLEY. Precisely.

CADRE. If you think that I would ever consent to becoming another one of your *puppets—*

LANGLEY. That would be uncomfortable, and above all, unnecessary.

CADRE. I refuse to recognize the fictional borders created by imperialist—

LANGLEY. Yes, yes, I know.

CADRE. By imperialists! Our struggle is international. Total.

LANGLEY. Save the rhetoric, you're talking to me now. *(slight pause)* All we really want is stability in the region.

CADRE. With certain "guarantees."

LANGLEY. Guarantees which you yourself will have to make to your own people, your interests, your allies.

CADRE. Such as?

LANGLEY. Economic reform.

CADRE. *(sardonic)* Preserve the wealth of those who have it, and mollify the discontent of those who don't?

LANGLEY. Mollify the "suspicions" of those who will lend you the money to sustain your power and effect your reforms.

CADRE. The Yanqui Bankers.

LANGLEY. And the Europeans. And the IMF. And the World Bank.

CADRE. And the accumulated fortunes from our misfortunes will be long gone — tucked away in Switzerland by way of the Caymans, Bahamas, and Panama!!

LANGLEY. With you and yours in power, believe me, where their cash has flown, they will follow. A small price to pay. *(long pause)*

CADRE. Why me?

LANGLEY. Who else?

CADRE. *(after another pause)* "Dollar diplomacy" will not keep me in check. ... You're going to have me on a leash!!

LANGLEY. A long leash. ... But, my friend, we are all on leashes. And sometimes, if the dog is big enough, strong enough, tenacious enough, he "leads" whoever holds the reins.

CADRE. *(after a slight pause, he grins)* Ah. Debt. ... Debt.

LANGLEY. You are very quick. Very shrewd.

CADRE. But, my "friend" ... Your current "puppets" tried this very thing. Their so-called "debt cartel."

LANGLEY. So they did.

CADRE. And when you could not make them dance to your command, you cut their strings.

LANGLEY. Whatever works.

CADRE. *(after a long pause)* Okay, Yanqui. Whatever works. *(LANGLEY starts to Exit.)* Wait.

LANGLEY. What?

CADRE. One more thing.

LANGLEY. Shoot.

CADRE. My predecossor.

LANGLEY. A problem?

CADRE. Yes.

LANGLEY. Done.

CADRE. You don't have to ... check first?

LANGLEY. Routine. *(Starts to Exit again, then stops.)* Just in case we hit a snag somewhere up the line, can you live with exile?

CADRE. Whose?

LANGLEY. His. Say ... Panama? Or Miami?

CADRE. No.

LANGLEY. Hmnnn.

CADRE. A problem?

LANGLEY. Probably not. Assuming you and the banks can work something out.

CADRE. And if we can't?

LANGLEY. Then ... you've got a problem. But I'm confident you'll come to terms.

(LANGLEY Exits, then returns with ROGERS. ROGERS is carrying a file. His nose is still banaged. ROGERS is not at all sure he likes having to deal with the CADRE.)

CADRE. So, we meet yet again.

ROGERS. So it seems.

LANGLEY. *(to ROGERS:)* Explain to our friend here what it is you have in mind.

ROGERS. Well ... *(Clears his throat.)* As you know ... *(Shuffles papers.)* The situation we have here is—

CADRE. *(cutting to the bone)* Considering the volatility of the current situation, with the government in transition and the time needed to reorganize on moral, equitable, *honest* grounds, I expect a moratorium on payments of my country's debts. *(ROGERS starts to object strongly, LANGLEY keeps him in check, nodding in the CADRE'S direction as if to say, "let him continue.")* A new schedule to be negotiated in good faith after six months; intermediate loans to facilitate the transition; all payments linked to GNP.

ROGERS. This is preposterous! How do we know he'll even be in power six months from now?!

LANGLEY. How about ... *(ROGERS and the CADRE both look to LANGLEY and wait for his suggestion. Pause.)* ... some refreshments? *(LANGLEY just smiles. The two men just look at him, slightly incredulous.)*

End of Scene 19

Scene 20
Photo Opportunity

The WOMAN sets up a microphone stand downstage. In another area of the stage, LANGLEY sits in front of a small TV set, his face washed by its glow. Crowd SOUNDS. The WOMAN tests the mike.

WOMAN. *Prueba. Prueba.* (Testing. Testing.)

(She steps aside, greeting NUEVA'S entrance with applause. NUEVA takes his place at the mike. Photo FLASHES. The strain in NUEVA's effort to speak perfect English is evident.)

NUEVA. Ladies and Gentlemen. Distinguished members of the Press. My friends. .... The civil unrest which has plagued our democratic republic for so many years is at an end. The so-called "people's revolution" has been crushed!!!

(Offstage SOUND of gunfire. NUEVA'S anxiety shows but he covers quickly with a broad confident smile.)

NUEVA. It is with great pleasure that I am able to announce the new agreement which I *personally* negotiated with ... the International Banks. *(NUEVA smiles, waiting for APPLAUSE. A smattering.)* The debt crisis has been averted. Our economy is finally secure. And growing.

(SOUND: More gunfire, screams.)

NUEVA. The guerrillas have been subdued, their backs broken, their organization in ... in shambles, their leaders discredited and exposed as ... exposed as ... Exposed!!

(SOUND: A bomb. NUEVA covers with a smile. After a moment, he continues.)

NUEVA. On the human rights front, our record is ... better than it has been in years. Our alliance with the United States is stronger than ever. Their faith in my leadership deeper than ever. Their trust in my ability, complete.

(The AUDIO begins to screech in horrible feedback when NUEVA resumes.)

NUEVA. The future of democracy is ... *(The SOUND system goes dead.)* The future of democracy ... *(NUEVA hits the microphone. Nothing.)* THE FUTURE OF DEMOCRACY IS SECURE! Thank you.

(LIGHTS out. SOUND of GUNFIRE which bridges into next scene.)

End of Scene 20

Scene 21

Big Fish, Little Fish (or, "My Dinner with Cadre")

ROGERS and NUEVA sit at opposite sides of a small table, turned away from one another. LANGLEY pours a glass of wine for each. The MAN, in a waiter's jacket, towel draped over his arm stands upstage, behind LANGLEY. SOUND of distant GUNFIRE offstage continues.

LANGLEY. When you've reached an agreement, contact me at the embassy. *(Starts to Exit. He stops next to the MAN.)* Oh, and don't worry about him. *(the MAN)* He's deaf, dumb, and — *(shouting suddenly into the MAN'S ear)* HAH!!

(The MAN doesn't flinch. LANGLEY smiles.) Bon Appetit. *(LANGLEY Exits. Slight pause. ROGERS and the CADRE take their glasses. The CADRE raises his glass in an intended toast, ROGERS raises his. Neither will make the opening.)*

ROGERS. To...

CADRE. Swaps.

ROGERS. Fine. To swaps then. *(They lift their glasses to their lips. Neither drinks. They sniff, swirl, sniff again, then set the glasses down. The MAN Exits. Another slight pause.)*

CADRE. Well, then.

ROGERS. Just who the fuck were you trying to impress with all that "moratorium, intermediate loan, GNP" crap back there? Me? If you were, don't bother. I've swum with sharks.

CADRE. And now you swim with piranha.

ROGERS. A hungry little fish.

CADRE. With *very* sharp teeth.

ROGERS. An inedible nuisance.

CADRE. And a voracious appetite.

(The MAN has Re-entered with a tray of hors ďouevres which he presents.)

ROGERS. Appetizer?

CADRE. *(examining then rejecting the selections)* Thank you.

ROGERS. Saving space for the entrée, amigo? *(ROGERS too decides against eating. The MAN draws back slightly.)* You say you're hungry, but for what? And don't give me a lot of psuedo-Marxist vox populi ding dong. ... This 's just you, me, and the bottom line. Let's make this short and sweet so I can get the fuck outa here, okay? ... Think of me as Santa Claus. Give me your list. I'll check it twice. I personally don't give a good goddam whether you've been naughty, nice, or just plain treacherous. *(pause)* Well?

CADRE. Between you and me?

ROGERS. Yeah. You and me. Our gracious host and the kitchen staff are long gone. *(The CADRE takes a moment before reaching under the tray and picking off an electronic "bug." He shows it to ROGERS, then drops it into the wine bottle. He grins. ROGERS grins.)* Not bad. For a piranha.

CADRE. *(mumbling) Camarero?* (Waiter?) *(The MAN, caught offguard, turns to the CADRE. No, he's not deaf, but he is now very anxious. The CADRE tips him then dismisses him. The MAN rushes out. After a slight pause.)* Swaps.

ROGERS. Debt for equity's a risky move. Long term. Then again, you may not be in this for the long term. You'll be selling off your country's assets at junk-shop prices.

CADRE. I know exactly what a debt-equity swap is and what it isn't. So, as you suggested, let's go to the bottom line. Your secondary market.

ROGERS. At the moment, there isn't one.

CADRE. *(after a slight pause)* Bolex International. Quincy Pharmaceuticals. Grey Chemicals. And ... BRX, wasn't it?

ROGERS. You've done your homework. Or has our host been gracious again?

CADRE. Our host believes I am a simple man with grand ambitions. Naive. Ignorant. Hypocritical. I have done nothing to correct this impression. In fact, I have encouraged it.

ROGERS. A man of principles.

CADRE. As you wish.

ROGERS. *(after a slight pause)* We can maybe dump about half your debt for about twelve cents on the dollar. *Maybe*. BRX and Bolex may be good for—

CADRE. A third. Grey'll take a bite, and with some luck and a nudge or two from one of your buddies in the State Department you may be able to twist Quincy's arm.

ROGERS. Buy-back in local currency through your national bank?

CADRE. Of course.

ROGERS. Grey'll want the mines and South harbor. Rail rights for fifteen years. BRX will be looking at a factory site on the river.

CADRE. Downstream from the capitol.

ROGERS. Waste's going to be a problem?

CADRE. How toxic?

ROGERS. Not much.

CADRE. But you wouldn't recommend drinking water from the river.

ROGERS. Hell, I wouldn't recommend drinking it *now!*

CADRE. And Bolex?

ROGERS. The usual.

CADRE. Cheap labor.

ROGERS. Very cheap.

CADRE. How cheap?

ROGERS. Can you match or better Mexico?

CADRE. Easily.

ROGERS. Good. That's good. One thing though...

CADRE. My finance minister.

ROGERS. You read my mind.

CADRE. My cousin.

ROGERS. Your lock?

CADRE. His cock.

ROGERS. Likes the ladies, does he?

CADRE. Boys. ... Young boys.

ROGERS. Wife?

CADRE. And family. Very proud. Very Catholic. Now, concerning the next six months to a year. An intermediate loan of say...

ROGERS. Two-fifty.

CADRE. Five.

ROGERS. Three's the best I can go.

CADRE. Three-fifty.

ROGERS. *(quickly)* Sold. ... How's your army?

CADRE. Small.

ROGERS. Loyal?

CADRE. Very.

ROGERS. Keep 'em close. And keep 'em in the dark.

CADRE. About?

ROGERS. BRX, Bolex, Grey and Quincy! Folks — especially the hungry folks with guns, glazed eyes, and a bunch of ideals — just do not know how the game is played. They might get the wrong idea. They might think you're selling off the family jewels, piece by piece — which, in fact, is exactly what you're doing.

CADRE. Bolex may own the river and Grey the mines but they can never take them home.

ROGERS. Talk like that will make the Bolex boys nervous. It makes *me* nervous.

CADRE. It should. *(They lock eyes. Long pause.)*

ROGERS. Dangerous game.

CADRE. Dangerous times.

ROGERS. For a piranha in the sea.

CADRE. Swimming with the sharks. *(slight pause)* Better that you should think of me as a remora fish. Feeding off the scraps, always inches from the shark's mouth. Small enough, fast enough, smart enough to fill its belly. Very safe. *(off ROGERS' look)* Who would dare attack a small remora swimming in the shadow of a shark?

ROGERS. Another shark.

CADRE. A shark is a shark is a shark. One is as good as another. Who says a smart remora must always stay loyal to the same shark? A bigger one swims near, I swim with him.

ROGERS. If you fuck with me or mine, you're...

CADRE. What? Fucked?

ROGERS. A forgotten footnote — never read, never even written. Bon appetit! *(ROGERS throws his napkin on the table then begins to Exit.)*

CADRE. When will you be back?

ROGERS. Too soon. And before I do...

CADRE. What?

ROGERS. Do something about your goddam golf course. Your greens suck.

End of Scene 21

Scene 22
Pulling Strings

MAHAN is alone in a dark, narrow room in a cheap hotel. NUEVA Enters quietly. Suddenly we hear the clatter of empty tin cans on the hard floor. MAHAN snaps his M16 at NUEVA who is untangling a string from his feet. The ends of the string are tied to the flip tops of two empty beer cans which had been standing at the bottom of two stacks of assorted cans.

NUEVA. It's me!

MAHAN. In another place and another time, those would've been Claymores.

NUEVA. And I would have been—

MAHAN. Dead. ... You might still be.

NUEVA. I need to talk to your boss.

MAHAN. The President?

NUEVA. You know damn well who I mean.

MAHAN. My orders come from the Commander in Chief, through the chain of command. My boss is the President of the United States. Go ahead, give him a call. He might not appreciate being woken up in the middle of the night but then again, neither do I.

NUEVA. The "Station Chief."

MAHAN. Oh, him. Why didn't you say so?

NUEVA. I'm saying so now. I can't find him.

MAHAN. Maybe he doesn't want to be found.

NUEVA. Why not?

MAHAN. Maybe he's got better things to do than hold your hand and whisper sweet nothings in your ear.

NUEVA. Something's happening. I feel it.

MAHAN. Something's always happening.

NUEVA. I hear rumors. I hear ... *(NUEVA approaches MAHAN'S cot with the intention of sitting down next to him. MAHAN stops him with a look and a way of his weapon.)*

MAHAN. Don't even think of it.

NUEVA. *(reacting)* I hear he's taken an important rebel leader captive. None of my people have seen either one of them. Where are they? *(MAHAN doesn't answer.)* And the Banker. No one's seen him either.

MAHAN. A few holes in your intelligence net? *(pause)* If I were you, I wouldn't go around telling people, any people, especially your people and most especially my people, that there are things you don't know and can't find out. Makes you look real bad, amigo. Incompetent. Cut out. Powerless.

NUEVA. *(after a long pause)* Help me.

MAHAN. How?

NUEVA. Arrange a meeting. A private meeting. Just him and me.

MAHAN. You and who?

NUEVA. The Station Chief dammit!!!

MAHAN. *(after a slight pause)* When?

NUEVA. Soon. As soon as possible.

MAHAN. What is it exactly you want to talk about with him?

NUEVA. You and I fought together!! We were allies! Friends! Compatriots in our cause!! Do these things count for nothing to you? He gave me his WORD!!

MAHAN. So what you're saying is you wanna talk "old times," sit around, shoot the shit, remind him of the good old days? *(NUEVA just glares at him.)* What you want to know is whether your stock's rising or falling. Right?

NUEVA. Yes.

MAHAN. Friend, if you gotta ask, you already got your answer. *(slight pause)* You got your meet, now get the fuck outa my room.

End of Scene 22

Scene 23
Dominos

A square wooden board sits on an upended ammo crate. On the board, pieces of a domino game have been set out, ready for play. Two chairs flank the makeshift table. After a moment, NUEVA Enters. He notes the domino game, takes a seat and pulls out a pack of Marlboros. The pack is empty. He crushes it and tosses it onto the ground. MAHAN Enters. NUEVA rises.

NUEVA. You said fourteen hundred hours!

(MAHAN says nothing. After a moment, he steps aside. LANGLEY Enters.)

NUEVA. I thought you had forgotten me.

LANGLEY. On the contrary. You have been greatly on my mind.

NUEVA. Like the country/western song.

LANGLEY. That's "Gentle on My Mind."

NUEVA. Ah.

LANGLEY. Sorry. *(LANGLEY dismisses MAHAN. MAHAN Exits. LANGLEY and NUEVA sit, the table between them.)* So...

NUEVA. So.

LANGLEY. You wanted to talk.

NUEVA. Yes. ... Has your associate told you—

LANGLEY. Nothing. Your meet, your agenda. *(another lengthy pause)*

NUEVA. Am I being displaced?

LANGLEY. In what way?

NUEVA. Has your government lost faith in my ability to lead?

LANGLEY. There have been some ... questions. Niggling doubts, really. Nothing unusual. Why?

NUEVA. I feel...

LANGLEY. Displaced?

NUEVA. On the periphery. Of events. Of ... strategy. Policy.

LANGLEY. I often feel the same way, my friend. The imagination is a terrible magnifier. *(NUEVA drops his eyes to the table. LANGLEY studies NUEVA closely. Finally.)* Why do you think we're here?

NUEVA. I asked and...

LANGLEY. No. ... The United States. Here. supporting you.

NUEVA. Contain Communism. *(no response)* Why else? *(with a big grin)* The climate? *(NUEVA watches LANGLEY carefully take his pieces and line them up in a standing row.)* Dominos.

LANGLEY. One falls, the others follow, right up the line through Mexico. *(LANGLEY flicks the endmost one with the nail of his little finger. They fall in classic fashion.)* According to the theory. We've been leaning on the friggin' theory in one form or another since 1910 — hell, since we took Puerto Rico from the Spanish.

NUEVA. And Texas from Mexico.

LANGLEY. That was pure expansion ... Russian style. *(LANGLEY smacks a piece onto the board.)* Twenty-five. ... A theory built on a metaphor — say, dominos — is a dangerous thing, it appears self-evident, therefore true. Your move. *(NUEVA again studies the configurations on the table. He starts to place his piece then hesitates. LANGLEY rapidly points out his options.)* That's five. There's six, eight, and seven. You could take the five, block my ten or set yourself up for another move. Why second guess me when you could play it safe? Then again, safe could lose the whole game. Your move. *(before NUEVA can place his piece)* "Strategic interests!!" Is that why you think we're here?

NUEVA. I ... I don't know, Senior.

LANGLEY. We've invaded Nicaragua, what, six times now? The first time to take over its National Bank, the last time, fifteen years' occupation. Then we bankroll the Somozas to mind the store and they rob us and everybody who touches them blind. ... In come the other guys. Who did all right, considering the bag of worms

Stazy left them. They got their kids reading, hospitals, food, got some of the fields back into production, a decent election...

NUEVA. Whose side are you on anyway?

LANGLEY. Play the friggin' game!!! *(NUEVA considers his next move.)* Truth is they've done a hell of a job. Admirable. If that's the kind of action you're looking for.

NUEVA. And you're not.

LANGLEY. I play ... dominos. Your move. We need a new base to work from. Salvador's a ... well Salvador's a fucking mess. Belize is dreaming of the day marijuana's legalized. It's either you or Honduras. A superpower's got to have a place to flex its muscle. Central America's our gym. Your move. *(NUEVA studies the configurations then, just before he is ready to make his play, LANGLEY grabs the piece from NUEVA's hand and smacks it decisively onto the table.)* There you get ten. Over here, though, you only get six, but four ends up in the pocket and two covers cost. Crunch the numbers this way, that way, play IMF against your friends and friends against enemies. A game of multiple possibilities. Not exactly dominos, not exactly banking. Call it ... You're not very good with the numbers, are you?

NUEVA. You mean...

LANGLEY. Economics 101.

NUEVA. For *that* I have advisors.

LANGLEY. Younger men. Guys who know the game, who love the game, who play the game — for keeps. So what is it?

NUEVA. *Perdone?*

LANGLEY. What's bothering you? Well?

NUEVA. The rebel leader whom I believe you have captured...

LANGLEY. Yes?

NUEVA. So you have taken him? *(no response)* Why wasn't I informed? *(again, no response)* Do you not trust me?! *(LANGLEY says nothing. Finally, LANGLEY reaches inside his coat. NUEVA draws a gun on LANGLEY. A long moment before LANGLEY slowly draws his hand from inside his coat. In his hand he holds a envelope and an airline ticket in a folder.)*

LANGLEY. What did you think I had? ... Your response suggests that it is you who does not trust *me. (Drops the envelope and ticket onto the table.)* Go on. Pick it up. It's yours. You earned it. *(NUEVA picks up the plane ticket.)* Now don't think of that ticket as economy class, think of it as ... a lower profile.

NUEVA. *(indicating the envelope)* My thirty pieces of silver?

LANGLEY. What makes you say that? Have you betrayed someone?

NUEVA. Have you? *(Suddenly, LANGLEY slams the edge of the table sending pieces of the game flying. NUEVA leaps to his feet, his gun still on LANGLEY. Who remains seated.)*

LANGLEY. American policy has two faces: bully and crybaby. We cry when we feel misunderstood or when we think no one likes us. We can't understand why *anybody* wouldn't like us — we do understand why everybody can, would, and should "envy" us — but "not like us?" Impossible! *(slight pause)* Hell, some'll like us, others won't. A grown-up America will finally accept that, for better or worse, a lot of the time, we are the bad guy. And bad guys actually like *not* being liked. And that, Jack, is what being "bad" is all about.

NUEVA. Like you?

LANGLEY. *(after a slight pause)* Define "democracy."

NUEVA. This is trick question, no?

LANGLEY. ANSWER THE QUESTION, SPIC!!!

NUEVA. "Democracy" ... is whatever keeps your gringo Congress happy enough to keep giving us money.

LANGLEY. *(Rises and applauds the answer.)* Not half bad. Perhaps I've underestimated you.

NUEVA. Perhaps you have.

LANGLEY. Though I doubt it. *(holding up the plane ticket)* Why do you refuse my gift?

NUEVA. Is it?

LANGLEY. From *mi casa* to *tu casa.*

NUEVA. After all these years you still do not speak my language.

LANGLEY. I think I do. *(Reaches into his coat again.)*

NUEVA. More? To ease a guilty conscience? You Americans think "money" solves all problems. I think that is what makes you such charming naive people. *(LANGLEY draws NUEVA'S chrome-plated revolver and levels it at NUEVA who snaps his weapon up at LANGLEY. Face off.)*

LANGLEY. A fine metaphor, don't you think? If I fire, you fire, we both die. ... A synecdoche of Mutally Assured Destruction. ... Sooner or later, one of us will have to trust the other. I challenge you to a duel of faith. *(Pause. Then LANGLEY turns his aim aside.)*

NUEVA. You are a very interesting man, Señor. Always playing games.

LANGLEY. Yes. I know. Someday ... well, we all have the capacity for change, don't we? *(LANGLEY lowers the gun to his side. NUEVA hesitates, then finally puts his gun on the ground and kicks it aside.)*

NUEVA. There! If you will shoot me, I am prepared to die! In my own country! On my own terms! Better to die at the hands of a man whom I respect than at the hands of an ant! *(LANGLEY snaps his gun up, training it on NUEVA'S heart. NUEVA clutches. LANGLEY slowly pulls the trigger. "CLICK." an empty round. LANGLEY laughs. NUEVA laughs.)* A fine joke.

LANGLEY. I thought you'd like it.

(When NUEVA starts to retrieve his gun, LANGLEY shoots him. NUEVA is stunned. He hovers a long moment before crumpling to his death. The CADRE and MAHAN Enter from opposite sides of the stage. They regard the dead General. LANGLEY crouches over NUEVA, finally placing the chrome-plated revolver on NUEVA'S chest. Flatly spoken:) "The King is dead; long live the King." ... So to speak. *(LANGLEY rises, reaching once again into his coat. This time he comes out with two large Havanna cigars.)* Oh, those Cubans ... *(LANGLEY hands one to the CADRE, the other to MAHAN. MAHAN sits and starts to light up. The CADRE makes a discreet "sign of the cross" over the dead General.)*

CADRE. *(to LANGLEY:)* About BRX. I have been talking to some of the *campesinos* who have farms on the river.

LANGLEY. Downstream from the capitol?

CADRE. Yes. And it's a big problem.

LANGLEY. You made the deal, not me.

CADRE. Children swim in that river. The women wash

clothes. So I'm going to have to tell BRX to take their plant, their plans, and their toxic shit someplace else. Maybe ... Shit Creek, West Virginia?

(MAHAN and LANGLEY laugh. Then suddenly, without warning, The WOMAN, having stolen into position behind the CADRE, plunges a knife/bayonet into his back. LANGLEY and MAHAN are both taken by surprise. And before either can act, The MAN Enters, shooting MAHAN twice.)

MAHAN. Shit. *(MAHAN falls, dying quickly. The MAN and WOMAN turn their weapons on LANGLEY. Pause. He turns first to the WOMAN.)*

LANGLEY. You dumb fuck!! YOU DUMB FUCKS!!! You just blew your one shot at making something out of your goddam revolution. *(LANGLEY grabs the dead CADRE and holds him up as illustration.) Muerto.* (Dead.) *Revolucíon, muerta.* (The Revolution, dead!) *(He lets the CADRE'S body fall.)* You really thought this through, I can tell. Who're you going to get now? Hunh?! Juan here? You gonna comb his hair, fix his teeth, fill his head with a bunch of half-assed ideas and plunk him in the palace?! Fuck it! Go ahead. Finish the job. Kill me! ... *Mata me!* (Kill me!) ... *Dispara!!* (Shoot!) *(He takes the WOMAN'S gun and places the barrel in his mouth. She pulls it away.)* DON'T GET FUCKING DECENT ON ME NOW! *(He turns to the MAN.)* Come on, Juan. You can do it. You're a man. SHOOT THE FUCKING GUN!!! *I WANT YOU TO KILL ME!! (The MAN won't. LANGLEY flips out completely — though it may be a ploy. Shocked by the simple human fact of being face to face with a madmad, the MAN and WOMAN lower their guns and watch LANGLEY pitch a full-fledged state-of-the-art fit. Finally, LANGLEY exhausts himself. The MAN once again takes aim on his face. LANGLEY gets to his knees, hands behind his head — classic POW position. Pause. LANGLEY turns to the MAN, looking right up the barrel into the MAN'S face.)* So, Juan ... are you familiar with the concept of debt for equity swaps?

(No response at all. Pause. The MAN and WOMAN "post" arms. The WOMAN picks up NUEVA'S plane ticket. She looks at it, looks at LANGLEY, then at the MAN, then LANGLEY again, then back at the ticket. She spits on the ticket then throws it on the ground in front of LANGLEY. LIGHT shift. The MAN and WOMAN Exit. LANGLEY, still on his knees, eventually drops his hands. He looks around him at the three dead men, the scattered pieces of the game. After another pause, LANGLEY reaches down and picks up the ticket. MUSIC up, LIGHTS fade.)

The End

COSTUME PLOT

ROGERS
(Scenes 1 & 2)
Dark blue business suit
Crisp white dress shirt
Striped tie
Highly polished dark shoes

(Scene 3)
Flowered tropical shirt
Light-colored slacks
De-cleated golf shoes
Golf cap

(Scenes 6, 7, 9, 10)
Same shirt as scene 3
Same slacks as scene 3
Dark shoes
Sunglasses

(Scene 12)
Same as scene 1 but coat is carried
Loosened tie
White handkerchief
White adhesive bandage on nose

(Scene 14)
Same as scene 12 but without coat

(Scenes 15, 19, 21)
Same as scene 14, coat worn

LANGLEY
(Scenes 1 & 2)
Dark suit
White shirt
Dark tie
Dark shoes & socks

(Scene 4)
Lightweight dark suit pants
T-shirt
White socks
Dark shoes
Bathrobe

(Scenes 6, 8, 12, 13, 15, 19, 20, 21, 23)
Lightweight dark suit
White socks
Dark shoes

(Scenes 6, 12)
Same as above, with sunglasses

(Scene 16)
Dark pants
Dark long-sleeved pullover
Dark nylon stocking pulled over face

MAHAN
(Scene 1)
Dark suit
Dark socks & shoes
White shirt
Dark tie
Sunglasses

(All other scenes)
Tropical military camouflage fatigues
Tropical combat boots
Canvas webbed ammunition belt
Headband
(in Scene 16) add dark nylon stocking face mask

NUEVA
(Scenes 2, 3, 13, 20)
Full dress general's khaki uniform with double epaulets, medals on both sides
Officer's dress hat
Khaki shirt
Dark tie
Dark socks & shoes
Sunglasses

(Scenes 5, 6, 8, 9, 17, 22, 23)
Same as above but without epaulets and medals. Add leather belt and holster for sidearm, sheath for knife.

CADRE
Dark pants
Dark shirt
Black military boots
Neckerchief
Dark ball cap
Fatigue jacket
Sunglasses
Canvas webbed ammunition belt
Bandolier of ammunition

(Scene 6)
Add brightly colored shawl

(Scenes 11, 14, 16, 18, 19, 21)
No sunglasses

(Scenes 18, 19, 21)
No bandolier, belt or cap

WOMAN
(Scene 3)
Cheap sandals
Baggy faded trousers
Tattered cloth serape
Oversized golf cap

(Scenes 5, 6, 7, 11, 16, 23)
Same as above without cap

(Scene 12)
Add tattered peasant's straw hat

(Scene 10)
Clinging dress, flouncy skirt
High heels
Earrings
Large bright-colored pocketbook

(Scene 17)
Baggy trousers (or underwear)
Well-worn faded halter top

(Scene 20)
Neatly pressed khaki blouse
Neatly pressed khaki slacks
Dark shoes

MAN
(Scenes 5, 9, 11, 16, 17, 23)
Baggy trousers, rolled up
Serape
Cheap sandals

(Scenes 6, 12)
Same as above but add tattered straw hat

(Scene 10)
Dark trousers, rolled up
Sandals
Guevara (lightly patterned shirt worn out)

(Scene 14)
Dark trousers, rolled up
Sandals
Dress shirt and tie
Suspenders
Glasses

(Scene 21)
Dark trousers, rolled up
Sandals
Dress shirt and tie
Red valet's jacket
White arm towel

PROPS AND WEAPONS PLOT

1. *Southern Exposures*
   Green-lined computer print-out
   Letter-sized envelope with cash

2. *Putting Around*
   Putter
   Golf ball
   Airline ticket in itinerary envelope
   Ballpoint pen

3. *Due Diligence*
   Large golf bag
   Full set of golf clubs
   Golf ball
   Chromed revolver (Nueva)*
   M16, knife in sheath (Mahan)

4. *The Other Economy*
   Bottle of San Miguel
   New York Times, front section
   Old-fashioned drink glass

5. *Rancho del Banco*
   Concertina wire
   Firewood
   Chromed revolver (Nueva)*
   M16, sheathed knife (Mahan)

6. *Yes, We Have Bananas*
   Shawls
   Dolls
   Money
   A banana
   Sidearm (Nueva)
   Chromed revolver (Woman)*
   MAC 10 automatic machine pistol (Cadre) (slung from rope)

7. *Name, Rank, and American Express Number*
   Golf ball
   Kerchief
   Rope
   Chromed revolver (Woman)*
   AK47 (Man)
   MAC 10, sidearm (Cadre)

8. *Double Espresso*
   Two demitasses
   Canvas bag
   Map drawn on paper
   Sidearms (Nueva and Mahan)
   MAC 10 (Cadre)

9. *Behind the "Veil"*
   Kerchief
   Rope
   Golf ball
   M16, garrot (Mahan)

AK47 (Man)
Sidearm, knife (Nueva)

10. *Drinks on the House*
Drinks with "umbrellas"
Lingerie
Money
Wallet
Chromed revolver (Woman)*

11. *Spoils of War*
Money
Canvas bag
Candle
Cigarette
Chromed revolver (Woman)*
MAC 10 and sidearm (Cadre)
AK47 (Man)

12. *Southern Air Transport*
Golfbag
Suitcase
Two burlap sacks
Attaché case
MAC 10 and sidearm (Cadre)

13. *After the Ball*
Cigarette
Matches

14. *P.S., Send Fresh Underwear*
    Telex machine or PC
    MAC 10 and sidearm (Cadre)

15. *Marionettes*
    Large envelope with blue border
    Briefing papers
    8x10 glossy photographs of Nueva and Cadre
    Telex print-out

16. *Nocturnal Visitors*
    MAC 10 and sidearm (Cadre)
    AK47 (Man)
    Chromed revolver (Woman)
    Knife (Langley)
    M16 (Mahan)

17. *Confiteor Omne Peccata Mea*
    Bare bedsprings
    Rope
    Knife (Nueva)

18. *The Big Picture*
    Cadre's kerchief used as blindfold
    Knife (Mahan)

19. *Let's Make a Deal*
    Briefing papers

20. *Photo Opportunity*
    Microphone
    TV set

21. *Big Fish, Little Fish,* or "My Dinner with Cadre"
    Wine bottle
    Two wine glasses
    Electronic bug
    Hors d'oeuvres tray

22. *Pulling Strings*
    Beer cans connected with string
    Two flashlights
    Sidearm (Nueva)
    Sidearm (Mahan)

23. *Dominos*
    Playing board
    Dominos
    Plane ticket in itinerary envelope
    Money envelope
    Two Havana cigars
    Empty Marlboro cigarette pack
    Chromed revolver (Langley)*
    Sidearm (Nueva)
    M16 (Mahan)
    AK47 with bayonet (Woman)
    Sidearm (Man)*

* Only two weapons must be able to fire: One sidearm and the chromed revolver.

DESIGN AND LARGE PROP PLOT

In the New York Off-Broadway production, the design and floor plan were kept simple in order to maximize playing area on a stage which was small and which had no side entrances. The wall which dominated Upstage had the appearance of washed and faded stucco with a niche-like window Stage Left of the door. The wall was topped with a coil of barbed wire. Hung behind and slightly above the wire, suspended in black, was the "news-jet" electronic display on which were displayed scene titles and moving stock quotations. All "sit-ables" and minimal stage furnishings were brought on and cleared by the actors during the blackouts between scenes. Below is a plot of these furnishings. For many scenes, no "furnishings" were used. "Hand props" are listed elsewhere in the "Props and Weapons Plot."

Scene 1
Hand props only.

Scene 2
Hand props only.

Scene 3
Hand props only.

Scene 4
Mahan sits in the one chair UL.

Scene 5
Man is entangled in a coil of "concertina wire" UC.

Scene 6
Man & Woman hawk wares arranged on blanket spread in front of them UR.

Scene 7
Rogers is seated, hands tied, in one chair C.

Scene 8
Nueva and Mahan open scene seated on small ammo crates placed DR.

Scene 9
Hand props only.

Scene 10
Small cafe table C.
Two chairs, side by side, RC.

Scene 11
One small ammo crate on which Cadre places candle, sidearm, and money C.

Scene 12
Hand props only.

Scene 13
One chair in which Langley sits, DC, facing the upstage door.

Scene 14

Table on which "telex" or PC rests UR, with one chair on which the Man sits to type facing R.

Scene 15

Hand props only.

Scene 16

Hand props only.

Scene 17

Bedsprings are swung to fill doorway UC.

Scene 18

Two chairs facing downstage, set UC.

Scene 19

Two chairs UC facing one another.

Scene 20

Two chairs UR. Langley sits in one facing DR, the TV sits on the other, facing Langley. Microphone stand is set DL by the Woman.

Scene 21

Small table with table cloth C, flanked by two chairs R and L.

Scene 22

Hand props only.

Scene 23
Domino board is set on a small ammo crate DR, flanked by two chairs facing one another.

Inventory
Two chairs—simple wooden chairs.
One small table.
Two small ammo crates.
A few pieces of firewood.
A coil of wire to simulate concertina wire.
A blanket.

NEWS SET
(SUSPENDED)

STUCCO WALLS

SIDE
WALLS
DRAPED
IN BLACK

(BLACK BORDER)

(BLACK BORDER)

(FLOOR: TREATED RUG PADS
DARK EARTH TONE

BASIC FLOOR PLAN
NEW YORK THEATRE WORKSHOP PRODUCTION
"DOMINO"

Other Publications for Your Interest

LAKEBOAT

(ADVANCED GROUPS—COMEDY)

By DAVID MAMET

8 men—Unit set

This fascinating series of vignettes, staged to great acclaim by the Milwaukee Repertory Theatre, is set aboard a Great Lakes steamer, bound from Gary to Duluth. It focuses in on the eight-member crew, the hardhats of the steel waterways, all but one of whom are "lifers." The other character is a young college man who has been hired to replace the night cook. He is the closest thing to the central figure. ". . . the show has much of Mamet's poetry of the inarticulate, the ritual, tribal double-talk that makes sense underneath the ludicrous patters of our lives."—Chicago Tribune. ". . . a banquet of meaty acting parts."—Milwaukee Sentinel. (#14017)

(Slightly Restricted. Royalty, $50-$35.)

GLENGARRY GLEN ROSS

(ADVANCED GROUPS—COMIC DRAMA)

By DAVID MAMET

7 men—2 Interiors

Winner of the London theatre equivalent of our Tony Award, this scalding comedy went on to take Broadway by storm, winning the Pulitzer Prize for drama in 1984. Never has Mr. Mamet's ear for the rhythms of actual, contemporary speech been more keen than in this tale of cutthroat real estate salesmen competing against each other for the money of unwary customers. One suavely vicious salesman, Richard Roma, is in the lead for the monthly sales award: a new Cadillac. Another, Shelly "The Machine" Levene, a former top salesman, is now riding a streak of bad luck on a smile and a shoeshine, hoping to turn his luck around. All are dependent upon an office manager named Williamson to give them the vital "leads" to new customers. Williamson, meanwhile, is pitting them against each other to drive up sales. In the first act, composed of three scenes, we meet the salesmen, vying for position as they gulp their cocktails in the local Chinese restaurant. The second act becomes a sort of "who done it" as the scene shifts to the office, where a burglary has taken place. The vital leads have been filched the night before, possibly by one of the salesmen. In the end, Williamson screws Roma out of his car and nabs the bag man. "Crackling tension . . . ferocious comedy and drama. A top American playwright in bristling form."—N.Y. Times. "Wonderfully funny . . . a play to see, remember and cherish."—N.Y. Post. "Mamet is . . . a pure writer, and the synthesis he appears to be making, with echoes from voices as diverse as Beckett, Pinter and Hemingway, is unique and exciting."—Newsweek. (#9058)

**(Restricted New York City and 100 mile radius.
Also restricted metropolitan Los Angeles, Philadelphia and New Haven.
Royalty, $60-$40.)**

Other Publications for Your Interest

THE BALLAD OF SOAPY SMITH

(ADVANCED GROUPS—EPIC COMIC DRAMA)

By MICHAEL WELLER

24 men, 9 women (with doubling)—Various interiors and exteriors (may be unit set)

"Col." Jefferson Randolph Smith, known as "Soapy" to his friends and foes, is a celebrated, notorious con man whose reputation has, alas, not preceded him to the Alaska Gold Rush town of Skagway in 1897, when the play takes place. Soapy is a charming gentleman, and he starts up a protection racket which brings law and order to the town, giving it a church and an infirmary. Oddly enough Soapy, the criminal, becomes a force for moral good; until the town's hypocrisy and vicious self interest bring him down, a victim of the cardinal sin of believing in his own con. "Michael Weller deserves praise for a historical play with contemporary relevance, daring to accost a large canvas. The protagonist is a complex and absorbing creation. I left the theatre, for once, thinking rather than trying to forget."—N.Y. Mag. "A rousing epic"—AP. "A good time on a grand scale, with a mind and vision of rare intensity."—Gannett/Westchester Newsp. (#3975)

(Slightly Restricted. Royalty, $60-40.)

HURLYBURLY

(ADVANCED GROUPS—DRAMA)

By DAVID RABE

4 men, 3 women—Interior

This rivetting new drama by the author of *The Basic Training of Pavlo Hummel*, *Sticks and Bones* and *Streamers* took New York by storm in a production directed by Mike Nichols and starring William Hurt, Sigourney Weaver, Judith Ivey, Christopher Walken, Harvey Keitel and Jerry Stiller. Quite a cast, and quite a play! The drama is the story of four men nosedeep in the decadent, perverted, cocaine-laden culture that is Hollywood; pursuing their sex-crazed, dope-ridden vision of the American Dream. "*Hurlyburly* offers some of Mr. Rabe's most inventive and disturbing writing. At his impressive best, Mr. Rabe makes grim, ribald and surprisingly compassionate comedy out of the lies and rationalizations that allow his alienated men to keep functioning (if not feeling) in the fogs of lotusland. They work in an industry so corrupt that its only honest executives are those who openly admit that they lie."—N.Y. Times. "Rabe has written a strange, bitterly funny, self-indulgent, important play."—N.Y. Post. "An important work, masterly accomplished."—Time. "A powerful permanent contribution to American drama . . . rivetting, disturbing, fearsomely funny . . . has a savage sincerity and a crackling theatrical vitality. This deeply felt play deserves as wide an audience as possible."—Newsweek. (#10163)

(Slightly Restricted. Royalty, $60-$40.)

Other Publications for Your Interest

THE CURATE SHAKESPEARE AS YOU LIKE IT

(LITTLE THEATRE—COMEDY)

By DON NIGRO

4 men, 3 women—Bare stage

This extremely unusual and original piece is subtitled: "The record of one company's attempt to perform the play by William Shakespeare". When the very prolific Mr. Nigro was asked by a professional theatre company to adapt *As You Like It* so that it could be performed by a company of seven he, of course, came up with a completely original play about a rag-tag group of players comprised of only seven actors led by a dotty old curate who nonetheless must present Shakespeare's play; and the dramatic interest, as well as the comedy, is in their hilarious attempts to impersonate all of Shakespeare's multitude of characters. The play has had numerous productions nationwide, all of which have come about through word of mouth. We are very pleased to make this "underground comic classic" widely available to theatre groups who like their comedy wide open and theatrical. (#5742)

(Royalty, $50-$25.)

SEASCAPE WITH SHARKS AND DANCER

(LITTLE THEATRE—DRAMA)

By DON NIGRO

1 man, 1 woman—Interior

This is a fine new play by an author of great talent and promise. We are very glad to be introducing Mr. Nigro's work to a wide audience with *Seascape With Sharks and Dancer*, which comes directly from a sold-out, critically acclaimed production at the world-famous Oregon Shakespeare Festival. The play is set in a beach bungalow. The young man who lives there has pulled a lost young woman from the ocean. Soon, she finds herself trapped in his life and torn between her need to come to rest somewhere and her certainty that all human relationships turn eventually into nightmares. The struggle between his tolerant and gently ironic approach to life and her strategy of suspicion and attack becomes a kind of war about love and creation which neither can afford to lose. In other words, this is quite an offbeat, wonderful love story. We would like to point out that the play also contains a wealth of excellent ***monologue*** and ***scene material.*** (#21060)

(Royalty, $50-$35.)

Other Publications for Your Interest

A MAP OF THE WORLD

(ADVANCED GROUPS—DRAMA)

By DAVID HARE

7 men, 4 women, plus extras—2 Interiors

This new play by the author of *Plenty* "is an ambitious work which brings together in heated discussion a young left wing journalist and a right wing expatriate Indian novelist. The settings are a Bombay hotel where they are attending a world poverty conference and the British film studio where the Indian author's experiences are being turned into a film. Throughout the play, life and fiction overlap . . . One of the issues is the sexual jealousy that arises over the men's competition for the favours of a promiscuous American actress staying at the hotel. Also on the agenda: idealism vs. cynicism; the West's arrogance in its handling of Third World problems; the alleged evils of Zionism; and the journalist's fervent belief in the necessity for change."—London Sunday Express. "It is a pleasure to hear a stage echoing to such issues and such talk."—London Standard. "A rich and complex play built around a series of antitheses: the Third World and the West, fiction and reality, irony and committment, reason and passion, the personal and the political. Yet for me what makes it the most mature and moving of Hare's works to date is its gut conviction that once we lose our Utopian dreams we have lost everything."—London Guardian. (#15620)

(Slightly Restricted. Royalty, $60-$40.)

NANAWATAI

(ADVANCED GROUPS—DRAMA)

By WILLIAM MASTROSIMONE

10 men, 1 woman, plus chorus of female extras—Unit set

The intrepid Mr. Mastrosimone, heretofore the author of studies of character such as *The Woolgatherer*, *A Tantalizing*, *Shivaree* and *Extremities*, has here set his sights on an epic scale. Shortly after the Soviet Union invaded Afghanistan, Mr. Mastrosimone managed to get himself smuggled into that beleaguered country via Pakistan. There he spent several weeks with the Afghani rebels, observing their often futile attempts to resist the Russian blitzkrieg. All of the resistance he witnessed was not futile, though; he also observed the capture and execution of a Soviet tank crew. It was this incident which inspired *Nanawatai* (an Afghani word which means "sanctuary"). The story is told through the dual points of view of a Russian tank crew member and an Afghani rebel, as a chorus of village women impresses upon us the effect on the citizenry of all the bloodshed (not unlike, of course, in a Greek tragedy). "Hard-hitting and probing . . . alive with issues and conflicts of both a political and personal nature."—Hollywood Reporter. "It has the ritual power of Greek tragedy."—L.A. Times. (#15975)

(Royalty, $50-$35.)